GLYN DANIEL

————◆————

MAN DISCOVERS HIS PAST

Bear, 15 cm. high, from the Neolithic grave at Samus in Siberia

GLYN DANIEL

MAN DISCOVERS HIS PAST

GERALD DUCKWORTH & CO. LTD.
3 HENRIETTA ST. LONDON, W.C.2.

First published 1966

Text © 1966 *by* GLYN DANIEL

PRINTED IN GREAT BRITAIN BY
UNWIN BROTHERS LIMITED
WOKING AND LONDON

To
PAUL and NANCY
in memory of *Animal, Vegetable, Mineral?*
and *Buried Treasure*

Contents

Preface

I have been lecturing on the history of archae-ology in Cambridge for a long time, and when Paul Johnstone asked me to do five half-hour television programmes on this subject in the B.B.C.'s further education series, I readily accepted this intriguing challenge to distil for a wider and less specialist audience what I had been saying to undergraduates for the last twenty years. The result was the series broadcast in the spring of 1966 and repeated in the autumn of the same year. It was directed by Nancy Thomas and produced by Paul Johnstone, and was recorded in my rooms in St John's College, and in those of Michael Wallington across the staircase, by kind permission of the Master and Fellows, and the ready co-operation of the Clerk of Works and his staff.

We decided not to broadcast from scripts and not to use jumbo-typed pini-prompters. This book is the monitored text of those unscripted talks. I have read through the transcripts kindly prepared by the B.B.C. and by my secretary, Mrs Eva Cousins, and in preparing the scripts for publication have done no more than take away phrases like "Here we have . . ." and "This is . . ." whose broadcast immediacy and relevance is unsuitable in the reading of the spoken word. I was disagreeably surprised to find how many of my sentences began with "now". These nows have been pared away from the text—and, I hope, from future lecturing and broadcasting.

The technique of recording was interesting. I tried out what I intended to say in the first ten minutes, then I took a short walk in the Backs, returned to my rooms and we made a recording of that ten minutes, and if it was no good another. The whole process took five days in December, 1965: it was a strenuous but rewarding week. One of the rewards was that while at the beginning of the week the B.B.C. technicians coping with the cameras and light and sound equipment in my rooms spent every spare moment reading maga-zines they had brought with them about minicars and bees and bungalows, at the end of the week they were reading archaeological books off my shelves: or do I delude myself, and it was just that the next edition of their magazines had not yet come out?

The B.B.C. have co-operated in the production of this book by providing many of the illustrations they used in transmission. Mr H. A. Shelley has drawn the maps as he drew the slightly different ones used in the programmes. I am particularly happy that this book should appear with the imprint of Gerald Duckworth and Company, because it was their Chairman, Mervyn Horder, who, by asking me in 1947 to write the volume on archaeology in their *Hundred Years* series, helped me develop my interest in the story of man's discovery through archaeology of his ancient past.

Glyn Daniel

St John's College, Cambridge
Ascension Day, 1966

List of Illustrations

The author and the publishers gratefully acknowledge the permission of the copyright holders, named in italics, to reproduce the illustrations in this book; also to Mr. Paul Johnstone and B.B.C. Educational Publications who helped to assemble the originals.

List of Maps

I. Stone, Bronze and Iron

Man is a historical animal, and it would be quite wrong of any of us to deny that this is so, and that all of us, in some way or another, are interested in some aspect of our own past. To some people their interests do not go far back—perhaps to their grandparents, to the 1914–1918 war, but to others the nineteenth century is almost contemporary with ourselves. The further back we go, more and more historical imagination is required. Queen Elizabeth the First is a long way back, and when we go further back still to the time of the Normans, the Anglo-Saxons, and eventually the Romans, we do really need a great exercise in historical imagination to discover our own past in those times.

When we go still further back to the time of the Ancient Britons, the people which the Romans found when they got to the British Isles, the exercise in historical imagination is more difficult still: this is for one main reason, that at that period of the past there are no sources except material sources—there are no written sources, archaeology is our only guide.

The first writing appeared in our country with the Romans, but of course writing itself is much older. The first writing we know of in the world occurred in Mesopotamia, in the south of Meso-potamia, in the land of the Sumerians. It was cuneiform writing, that is to say it was done by wedge-shaped marks made with the end of a reed or stylus cut diagonally. This is the first writing and it begins the whole of history in the strict sense—history based on written sources. But this was only just over five thousand years ago—three thousand to three thousand five hundred years B.C. If we take the most conservative estimates for the life of Man, that is *Homo sapiens*, he has been in existence for between a half to three quarters of a million years. People have often given the figure of 600,000 years and if you think in terms of a clock-face representing 600,000 years, then writing occurred only in the last half-minute of time during which *Homo sapiens* has been in existence; a sobering thought.

It is man's long pre-written past that we are trying to discover through archaeology. We have to do this by studying the pots and pans and implements that man left behind; tools and implements of copper and bronze were made before man had any knowledge of iron, and stone implements—polished and chipped—before man had any knowledge of working metal at all. The primitive chipped implements go back to the very remotest past of man [1].

To most people archaeology is excavation. The first excavator we know about is an Assyrian

1. Mesopotamian Cuneiform writing

princess of the sixth century B.C. She was a collector, and with the assistance of her father, dug about in the ruins of a much earlier civilisation—that of the Sumerians [2]. The Greeks who inherited, among other things, the learning of the most ancient Near East, were not very interested in the past, except as travellers—and they did not excavate [3]. Excavation is something that dates from the last two hundred and fifty years. In the late middle ages and the Renaissance in western Europe we have people who, while interested in the past, do not excavate. They prefer to invent the past. A good example of these mediaeval antiquaries is Geoffrey of Monmouth whose *Historia Regum Britanniae* was published in the twelfth century. Geoffrey wanted to connect the origins of the British with the Trojans and he brought Brutus, a Trojan prince, to Great Britain. He made him land at Totnes, in South Devon in 1170 B.C., and of course alleged that the name of Britain came from this eponymous hero Brutus [4]. My own University of Cambridge also wanted to have a fine past, and was prepared to invent it, and so there was created a remarkable person called King Cantaber, who never existed: he was made to set off from the East Mediterranean and travel to Britain via Spain—he left his name in Cantabria—and eventually arrived here and founded the city and University of Cambridge [5].

Of course all this was nonsense, but it was all that people had to think about in early mediaeval times. They could only invent the past. The real discovery of the past starts with the antiquaries of the sixteenth, seventeenth and eighteenth centuries—with men like the Wiltshire squire John Aubrey, who first gave full descriptions of Stonehenge and Avebury: Lytton Strachey called him the "first British archaeologist" [6]. This title could be shared by my countryman, Edward Lhwyd, or a man like William Stukeley. I take Lhwyd as a particularly interesting example of these first antiquaries not because, like myself, he was a Welshman spending his life in one of the two great old Universities of England, but because he did travel more widely than Aubrey or Stukeley. He was Keeper of the Ashmolean

2. Stukeley's drawing of Stonehenge

Museum at Oxford, and while there arranged to make very extensive travels lasting over five years in Wales, Scotland, Ireland, Cornwall and Brittany. On the way, while he was in Brittany, sitting at a table with lots of notes trying to understand the relation of the Breton language to Welsh and Irish, he was apprehended. as a spy, and spent three weeks in prison in Brest before he was sent back to Oxford [7].

He made good drawings and plans, and a few years after his return to Oxford he published the first volume of his long expected work entitled *Archaeologia Britannica*. Alas he didn't live long enough to produce the next few volumes: his dates were 1670 to 1709. Men like Aubrey, Lhwyd and Stukeley were trying hard to do the best they could with the sources they had: although they looked at ancient monuments their main sources were written sources—the Bible and classical writers. It is therefore not surprising that the Druids appear a great deal. William Stukeley in the second half of his life really suffered from Druidomania, and although he was himself a good antiquary and recorded Stonehenge and Avebury with great care, he peopled these ancient and remarkable monuments entirely with Druids. We must not be too critical of him: this is all people could do at the time, until they began to excavate [8]. In this country excavation began in the eighteenth century and we may take as good examples of the late eighteenth and early nineteenth century excavators, two men who worked in Wiltshire—William Cunnington and Sir Richard Colt Hoare.

William Cunnington described himself digging barrows on Salisbury Plain in 1803 "in the hopes of meeting something which might supersede conjecture" and in his *Ancient Wiltshire* Colt Hoare said "we speak from facts not theory. I shall not seek among the fanciful regions of Romance an origin of our Wiltshire barrows." They were trying by their excavations to discover the correct truth about the past; and this archaeology in the later nineteenth century and the twentieth century succeeded in doing. But Colt Hoare still had the flavour of the past, of the earlier antiquarians, and we find him saying of a skeleton he found that it "was grinning horribly a ghastly smile . . . a singularity I have noticed before." Cunnington and Colt Hoare were trying by excavation to arrive at the facts about the past. There were some people who said this was impossible; one of them was Dr Johnson, who wrote "All that is really known of the ancient state of Britain is contained in a few pages. We can know no more than what old writers have told us." But in this, as in many other matters, the great Dr Johnson was wrong.

Yet, in spite of their hard work and their devotion to archaeology, men like Cunnington and Colt Hoare, working hard at excavation as they did, could not find a way through. Everything they touched remained stubbornly Ancient British. Colt Hoare confessed that his aim was "to ascertain to which of the successive inhabitants of this island" the prehistoric antiquities "are to be ascribed, or whether, in fact, they are the work of more than one people." But after ten years' work trying to produce a time-scale—

some depth—into the picture of pre-Roman Britain, and pre-Roman Europe, he was forced to confess to "total ignorance as to the authors of these sepulchral memorials: we have evidence of the very high antiquity of our Wiltshire barrows, but none respecting the tribes to whom they appertained, that can rest on solid foundations."

It began to look as if Dr Johnson was right—that excavation could not find a way through to produce a system of the past which would replace the guesswork of the earlier antiquaries. There was at the same time the same feeling in Denmark. Rasmus Nyerup, Professor of History in the University of Copenhagen, who was charged with the care of the Royal Cabinet of Curiosities and the task of converting it into the National Museum of Denmark, was also faced with this problem of how to arrange the things in the museum, so that they made some kind of sense of the prehistory that lay behind the history of Denmark. He could find no way of doing this and we find him saying "All that has come down to us from Heathendom is wrapped in a thick fog; it belongs to a space of time that we cannot measure. We know that it is older than Christendom, but whether by a couple of years or by a couple of centuries, or even by more than a millennium, we can do no more than guess."

What was needed was something to replace these guesses—the guesses of the mediaeval antiquaries, the guesses of the seventeenth- and eighteenth-century antiquaries looking at written sources as the only source, and the hard-won but seemingly ineffective guesses of the people who were now trying to excavate the past. You may well ask, how could there be a new system to replace the old? It happened, and it happened for three reasons. The first was the recognition that there existed stone implements made and fashioned by man. Flint implements had been found by farmers and gardeners and gravel-diggers for many centuries, and the widespread explanation of them was that they had been made by supernatural beings—fairies or elves; indeed some of these early flint implements were called "elfshot." The first change in thinking was the realisation that these things were not made by fairies and elves, were not the work of super-natural beings, but were made and fashioned by man. The earliest record of this new belief in England was that of Sir William Dugdale, the historian of Warwickshire, who, in the seventeenth century said of these stone implements, "These are weapons used by the Britons, before the art of making arms of Brass or Iron was known." Later, when sending a parcel of stone implements to the Society of Antiquaries of London, Charles Littleton, Bishop of Carlisle, said—his letter is published in *Archaeologia*, the main journal of the Society, in 1773—"There is not the least doubt of these implements having been fabricated in the earliest times by a barbarous people, before the use of Iron or other metals was known."

Here then we have people arguing from objects, from artifacts, that there had been a Stone Age. The second reason was even more cogent. Primitive peoples living in a stone technology have been observed by people travelling the world from the ages of discovery onwards. America and Africa revealed stone-using people ignorant of metallurgy, and this produced philosophical discussion: it was said that if people used stone implements, they must have been ignorant of metal—if not, why should they use stone and flint? This philosophical argument was clearly set out by the Danish historian Vedel Simonsen, who in the first years of the nineteenth century wrote a history of Denmark in which he said that in the past of man there were three ages, a Stone Age, then a Brass or Bronze Age, and then an Iron Age. Vedel Simonsen had suggested that there were successive periods in the prehistoric past.

But the third reason was the demonstration by archaeological means of these three periods. Nyerup was succeeded as Curator of the Danish National Museum by a young man called Christian Jurgensen Thomsen—a very important figure in the history of archaeology. Thomsen organised the collections in Copenhagen into a new museum and in 1819 it was opened to the public. He was very assiduous in showing visitors around. What the visitors found when they got into the Danish National Museum was that it was arranged into a Room of Stone, a Room of Bronze, and a Room of Iron. The philosophical speculations had now become a museum-ordering. Thomsen enlisted as his assistant a brilliant and dedicated young man called Jan Jacob Rasmussen Worsaae. Worsaae has been described as the first professional archaeologist in the world, and so he was, since Thomsen was a well-to-do merchant who had devoted first his leisure and then all his time to archaeology. Unlike Thomsen, Worsaae was not only interested in the Museum; he was also interested—which Thomsen was not —in excavation. He excavated extensively in his native Jutland, and often with special advantages; his friend the King of Denmark provided him with a platoon of soldiers to assist in his field-work.

3. King Frederick VII of Denmark and J. J. A. Worsaae on an excavation in Jutland

What Worsaae did was to show in his excavations that what had been a philosophical speculation and a museum-ordering was in fact historical truth as revealed by the stratigraphy observed in excavations. He was actually one of the first persons to record different stratigraphical levels [9]. Although he was scientific in many ways, he had not entirely thrown off the mantle of the eighteenth century romantic archaeologist: it seems to us incredible that he could have found anything like the scene depicted in figure 5, and by the way, I allege I see here the ghastly smiles which were grinned horribly by ancient skulls according to some eighteenth-century scholars. Worsaae is halfway between the romantic antiquarians of the eighteenth century and the highly organised and purposeful archaeologists of the late nineteenth century. He was halfway from the romantic past out of which he had grown and the scientific future which he was creating.

It may well be asked, was this happening only in Denmark? and the answer is no. In the dry summers of the middle 1850s, the water in the Swiss lakes dropped to hitherto unobserved low levels, and there were revealed, to the surprise of many, piles of wood sticking out of the water and rafts of wood—what we now refer to as the classic Lake Dwellings of Switzerland and elsewhere. Now what was interesting from our present point of view is not merely the discovery of Swiss Lake Dwellings, although they were very interesting, nor the fact that they preserved so much of special interest from the past, but that here again was demonstrated stratigraphically by excavation the technological succession of Stone, Bronze and Iron [10]. Worsaae himself said that the Three Age system of successive ages of Stone, Bronze and Iron which Thomsen devised in the Museum at Copenhagen was the first clear ray shed across the universal prehistoric gloom of the North and for that matter, of the European world in general. These may seem rather extravagant words, but we know what Worsaae means: something had happened which cut through the fog of

4. C. J. Thomsen showing to the public the National Museum of Antiquities in Copenhagen, or the Old Nordic Museum as it was called when this drawing was made in 1846

which Nyerup had despairingly spoken. A system for the prehistoric past had been produced—a system which worked for northern Europe and had been shown to work also for Switzerland.

The Danish National Museum published in 1819 a guide to its collections, and the guide to the prehistoric part was based on the Three Age system [11]. This guide was translated into English by Lord Ellesmere and published in 1847: here for the first time was available to the people of England a summary of the new system of prehistory—they could no longer complain that they could not read Danish and therefore did not know what it was all about. Worsaae himself wrote a general guide to Danish prehistory, using the Museum classification and his work in the field; this too was translated into English by W. J. Thoms under the title of *Primeval Antiquities of Denmark* (1849). So in the third quarter of the nineteenth century, the Three Age System, which was to be such an important element in our appreciation of the prehistoric past, was available in English to us.

The man who was really responsible for popularising the idea of successive technological ages in the prehistoric past of man was a man

N   S

5. Worsaae's drawing of skeletons found in a megalithic tomb in Jutland

born as John Lubbock, who subsequently became Sir John Lubbock, and eventually when he was made a peer took the title of Lord Avebury—when this happened one of his friends, or possibly one of his enemies, asked "And how long do we have to wait until he becomes Viscount Stonehenge?" He never became that and died in the fullness of time as Lord Avebury. He found time in his life to do an enormous variety of things: he was a merchant banker, a scientist, and yet was able to write many general books on the utilisation of leisure, what to read, how to be happy, and two books on prehistoric archaeology. One of his main claims to fame, which most people have forgotten, is that he invented Bank Holidays—they were for a short time called John Lubbock Days—and ought still to be so called, in my view. His first archaeological book was *Prehistoric Times* which came out in 1865—a hundred years ago. The full title is *Prehistoric Times illustrated by Ancient Remains, and the Manners and Customs of Modern Savages*. It was, and is, a very fine book. It introduced the words *prehistoric* and *prehistory* into the English language—they had been used before, but not generally used. It also set out a new idea—the extension of the Three Age System [12].

Lubbock had travelled not only in Denmark, but also in France and of course southern Britain, and he was well aware of the archaeological work in France, which we shall be discussing in the next talk—namely the finding of chipped flint implements in the gravels of the Somme. He realised that here in these chipped flints there was a very different kind of stone age from the stone age represented by the polished stone implements found in Scandinavia and elsewhere. He proposed that the Stone Age be divided into two parts which should be called the Old or Older Stone Age and the New or Newer Stone Age; but he wanted these two phases to have rather technical names, and so he invented the neo-Greek words *Palaeolithic* and *Neolithic*—these do not occur in ancient Greek; they are Lubbock's neo-grecisms. And so the system of the Three Ages of Man begun in Denmark in the early nineteenth century became the Four Age System in 1865—

the system as modified by Lubbock—Palaeolithic or Old Stone Age, Neolithic or New Stone Age, Bronze Age, and Iron Age.

There can be no doubt that this system was, for the next half century and more, the basis of our discovery of Man's past. If it had not been developed we could not have got any further. If it had not penetrated through the fog and gloom, we should be still in them. Déchelette, the great French prehistorian, regarded it as the basis of all prehistory, and Professor R. A. S. Macalister called it the "corner-stone of modern archaeology." These words were quite right, but it took a long time to persuade some people that this was so. [13]

Let us take the official attitude of the British Museum as a case in point. When the British Museum started in the middle of the eighteenth century, it had only three departments—printed books, manuscripts, and natural history—but gradually it began to study the antiquities. Yet when its first guide was produced there was nothing at all in it about British or Roman antiquities. This was in 1851, and the Guide said this was "because at present they are too insufficiently arranged to admit of classification and description." Remember that this was in 1851, a good 30 years after the National Museum at Copenhagen had been opened to the general public, arranged on the three-age system. In 1866 Franks, later Sir Augustus Franks, became the first Keeper of the new department of British and Medieval Antiquities at the British Museum, and he decided that he would arrange his material according to the system of the Northern Antiquaries. The antiquities were set out in 42 cases, and labelled according to the system. The *Guide to the Exhibition Rooms*, which he published, says that "The remains of the people of the British Islands previous to the invasion of the Romans were set out according to the Stone, Bronze, and a portion of the Iron Age of the Northern Antiquaries." Note that phrase "of the Northern Antiquaries", not of all history. And he goes on,

"They have for convenience been classed according to their materials and in the order corresponding to that of the supposed introduction of these materials into this country"—a pretty damning way of dealing with the situation. But the real point is that in 1866 this system had actually penetrated into the British Museum.

From then on, this system, the Three Age System of Scandinavia, and the Four Age System of Lubbock, became the universal system of prehistory. We talk about models of thought about the past; this was a technological model based on the materials used for making cutting tools. It was the model used by prehistorians until very recently. We are now discarding it because we have new models and because it has served its purpose. But it was the fundamental pattern in the nineteenth century, though modified from time to time. The main modification was the introduction of a fifth age—called by another neogrecism, the *mesolithic*—between the Old Stone Age and the New Stone Age. So that by 1900 the old Danish Thomsen system was Palaeolithic, Neolithic, Mesolithic, Bronze Age, Early Iron Age.

This brings us to the end of the nineteenth century. Let us just go back and remind ourselves of the stages in the development. First of all there was nothing, no system—only fog and gloom and guesswork. Then the system of ages was proposed as a philosophical doctrine and then—the most important element in the development of the system—it was used practically by Thomsen in the Copenhagen Museum. Next it was shown to be correct in the field by Worsaae in Jutland and Swiss archaeologists digging in their Lake Dwellings. Then it was extended: people like Lubbock and others realised that while it had started as a good system it needed extension and so it grew into a Four Age System and a Five Age System. But all the while it was the basic idea of Stone, Bronze and Iron that had illuminated, in Worsaae's words, the gloom that had hitherto gathered around our knowledge of the early past.

II. The Antiquity of Man

The Three Age system which we discussed in the first talk, and saw developing into the Four Age System and the Five Age System, gave a key to the past—a key in depth—but it did not produce actual dates. And this was a question in which people became very interested. Granted there was a Stone Age, or two Stone Ages, what were their dates; how old were these periods in the past of Man in North-west Europe and Scandinavia and Switzerland? Here was the second problem that exercised the nineteenth-century archaeologists.

First, what was the answer that had been provided hitherto? It was an answer provided by divines of the sixteenth and seventeenth centuries who, like the antiquaries of the same time, had only written sources to rely on. But whereas the antiquaries concentrated on the Druids and Classical writers which gave them nothing about chronology, the divines concentrated on the Bible, and particularly on the *Book of Genesis*. You will remember that in *Genesis* there are accounts of people who lived for a very long time —rather longer, it seems to many of us, than is the expectancy of life in these modern days. Certain theologians thought that if they used these tables, and added them up, they could work back from historical events to the date of the Flood and eventually the date of the Creation of the World. One of these was Ussher, a Civil War prelate who became Archbishop of Armagh. In 1650 he published his *Annals of the Ancient and New Testaments:* it was very widely read. In it he put forward the date of 4004 B.C. for the origin of the world and therefore, of course, the origin of Man. It was this sort of date that enabled Sir Thomas Browne to say "Time we may comprehend. 'Tis but five days elder than ourselves, and hath the same horoscope with the world" [*15*].

There were some people who felt that this date was not sufficiently accurate; one of them was Dr John Lightfoot, who was Master of St Catharine's College, Cambridge and later Vice-Chancellor of the University. He wrote a book called *A few and new observations on the Book of Genesis, the most of them certain, the rest probable, all harmless, strange and rarely heard of before.* In it Lightfoot said "Heaven and earth, centre and circumference were created all together and in the same instant, clouds full of water. This took place, and Man was created by the Trinity on the 23rd October, 4004 B.C. at 9 o'clock in the morning." I sometimes think that here we have the prejudice of a Vice-Chancellor for what is normally the beginning of an Academic Year, and what is, for at least some people, the beginning of the academic morning. But that is neither here nor there: what is important is that there was an idea of a world that was not more than six thousand years old, that is to say four thousand years before Christ and two thousand years afterwards. The idea that one could understand a world of six thousand years became common. People did not necessarily believe in the 23rd of October at 9 o'clock in the morning, but they did believe that the past was short. This is how one can explain, if the world was only six thousand years old, the line in Burgon's poem about Petra "A rose-red city 'half as old as time'." Time was six thousand years, half was three thousand years, and Burgon was trying to say that Petra was 1000 B.C. [*16*]. There was here a perfectly reasonable and factual way of describing things, if of course you believed in 4004 B.C.

Then gradually, in the late eighteenth century,

evidence began to accumulate which suggested that all was not easily to be explained within the span of a system of six thousand years. Meanwhile the year 4004 B.C. had been put in the margins of the Authorised Version of the Bible and soon seemed to many people to have the same authenticity as Holy Writ itself. The date was read in the margins of *Genesis* and thought to be divinely inspired. But doubts began to grow at the end of the eighteenth century. In 1771 a German, Johann Esper, discovered human bones associated with cave bear and other extinct animals in a cave near Bayreuth. He described them in 1774 and asked himself—and his readers—this question: "How am I to explain these things within the limits of our certain knowledge?" He said of these finds "Did they belong to a Druid or to an Antediluvian or to a Mortal Man of more recent times?" These were the three categories in which a man like Esper could think in the eighteenth century. Were the remains he found something to do with the Bible, therefore before the Flood, or something to do with Classical writers, who wrote about Druids, or were they in neither of these categories, but something modern? Esper comes to this conclusion: "I dare not presume"—an interesting

phrase, is it not?—"I dare not presume without any sufficient reason these human members to be of the same age as the other animal petrifactions. They must have got there by chance together with them." One can almost see him arguing the case with himself [17].

That was in 1771, and the words I have quoted were published in 1774. Thirty-three years later, in 1797, a gentleman farmer of Hoxne in Suffolk, near Diss across the county border in Norfolk, by name John Frere wrote a letter to the Secretary of the Society of Antiquaries of London, describing some interesting things that he had found. His letter was published in volume thirteen of *Archaeologia*, in 1800. "Sir, I take the liberty to request you to lay before the Society some flints found in the Parish of Hoxne, in the county of Suffolk, which, if not particularly objects of curiosity in themselves, must, I think be considered in that light from the situation in which they were found. They are, I think, evidently weapons of war, fabricated and used by a people who had not the use of metals. They lay in great numbers at a depth of about 12 feet in a stratified soil, that was dug into for the purpose of raising clay for bricks. The situation in which these remains were found may tempt us to refer them

THE FIRST BOOK OF MOSES,

CALLED

GENESIS.

CHAPTER 1.

1 The creation of heaven and earth, 3 of the light, 6 of the firmament, 9 of the earth separated from the waters, 11 and made fruitful, 14 of the sun, moon, and stars, 20 of fish and fowl, 24 of beasts and cattle, 26 of man in the image of God. 29 Also the appointment of food.

IN the *a*beginning *b*God created the heaven and the earth.

2 And the earth was *c*without form, and void; and darkness *was* upon the face of the deep. *g*And the Spirit of God moved upon the face of the waters.

B.C. 4004.
a John 1.1, 2.
Heb. 1. 10.
b Ps. 8. 3.
& 102. 25.
Is. 44. 24.
Acts 17. 24.
Rev. 4. 11.
c Ps. 136. 8.
1 Heb. *for the rule of the day.*
d Ps. 8. 3.
e Jer. 4. 23.
f Job 38. 7.
g Is.40.13,14.

the night; and let them be for signs, and for seasons, and for days, and years:

15 And let them be for lights in the firmament of the heaven to give light upon the earth: and it was so.

16 And God made two great lights: the *c*greater light *1*to rule the day, and *d*the lesser light to rule the night: *he made* f*the stars also.

17 And God set them in the firmament of the heaven to give light upon the earth,

18 And to *h*rule over the day and

6. "B.C. 4004" entry from the Authorised Version of the Bible

7. John Hookham Frere

8. Flint handaxe found at Hoxne in Suffolk

to a very remote period indeed, even beyond that of the present world."

Here is a contrast between two men writing at about the same time: Esper saying "I dare not presume. . . . They must have got there by chance" and Frere saying "A very remote period indeed, even beyond that of the present world." It is perfectly clear what Frere meant by "the present world": it was the world as understood in 1797 and 1800, 'cabin'd and confin'd' to six thousand years. This gentleman farmer of Suffolk began asking himself "Can this be so? Is the life of man, and the life of the world, as short as we have been told it is by the theologians of the sixteenth and seventeenth centuries." In a word Frere was saying to himself "Has the date 4004 B.C. on the margins of the Authorised Version of the Bible got the authenticity of Holy Writ itself?" There is no record that the Society of Antiquaries paid much attention to his letter; no one did much about it until sixty years later in 1859, after new discoveries had been made in France and in Devon, and it was realised that John Frere's observations were correct and important.

When Frere referred his finds at Hoxne to a time beyond that of the present world he naturally had to think what he meant by this phrase, and

he did add this sentence to his letter; "Whatever our conjectures on that head may be, it would be difficult to account for the stratum in which they lie being covered with another stratum which on that supposition may be conjectured to have once been the bottom or at least the shore of the sea." This difficulty had already been faced and met by some people in England—the new science of *geology* was often referred to in the late eighteenth and early nineteenth century as "the English science." The first person to deal with this problem in a new and scientific way was James Hutton whose *Theory of the Earth* was published in 1785: there he says quite clearly, anticipating the doctrine that was called in the nineteenth century the doctrine of uniformitarianism—not, I hasten to make clear, unitarianism—"No processes are to be employed that are not natural to the globe . . . No action to be admitted except those of which we know the principle." That is to say no wonders, no miracles, no universal floods, but processes in the past only similar to those we can see going on at the present day. That was James Hutton. The second person who helped to organise the new English science of Geology was William Smith—Strata Smith as he was called; his book, published in 1816 was entitled *Strata identified by organised fossils.* Hutton and Smith were providing the explanation that Frere wanted.

They were in advance of their time. The early nineteenth century was still dominated in the geological world by people who believed in the old geology, and one of the best examples of these was William Buckland. His dates are 1784 to 1856; he was a don at Christchurch, the first Professor of Geology in Oxford, indeed the first person to hold such a post in any British university. He was of course an Anglican priest, and subsequently became Dean of Westminster. His great book was published in 1823, and it was called *Reliquiae Diluvianae or Observations on the Organic Remains contained in the Caves, Fissures,* *and Diluvial Gravel and on other Geological Phenomena attesting the action of a Universal Deluge.* This was the doctrine of the older geologists, a doctrine based on wonders and miracles, catastrophes and universal floods, a doctrine which did not believe in the steady accumulation of deposits in a uniform way is what Hutton and Strata Smith were proposing. It was once said in a parody of Pope:

> Some doubts were once expressed about the
>   Flood,
> Buckland arose and all was clear as mud.

This is however what Buckland did do in the early nineteenth century. Every time some evidence appeared he muddied it because he was

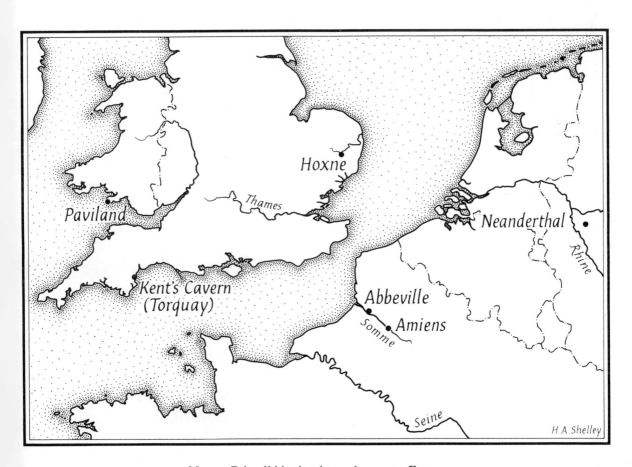

Map 1. Palaeolithic sites in north-western Europe

23

9. William Buckland

decided they were the remains of a woman, they have always been referred to as "The Red Lady of Paviland." These bones are now in the Pitt-Rivers Museum in Oxford. Buckland had to explain away this skeleton, found apparently in association with Palaeolithic tools. He decided that the apparent association must be due to an accident—some disturbance from a later date. On the top of the cliff he found what we would now call an Early Iron Age camp. Buckland decided it was a Roman camp, and decided that what had happened was that on a dark night a Roman soldier had taken out a native girl, knocked her on the head, and buried her in the cave. One thing was certain: the head of the Red Lady of Paviland was missing so the detail of the end of this person could not be decided. But apart from all this, here was Buckland's explanation. It is a good example of what he did at all times when difficult evidence came to light in Devon or

thinking in terms of the Bible. Just as the sixteenth and seventeenth century divines thought that the only explanation of chronology was in terms of the Bible, here the only explanation of geology was in terms of the Bible. As the only great catastrophe in the Old Testament was the Flood, then the explanation of geology was in terms of a Universal Flood!

But Buckland was put on the spot on several occasions. In 1823 he was himself excavating in Derbyshire when he heard of a discovery at the Goat's Hole Cave at Paviland on the coast of the Gower Peninsula in south Wales. What he heard from south Wales was so interesting that he went off himself and excavated it.

He found there the remains of a person—and I deliberately say "a person" because Buckland himself thought it was the remains of a young lady, though subsequently it has been shown to be the remains of a young man. The bones were covered with red ochre, and since Buckland had

10. Sir Charles Lyell

Wales or anywhere else. He muddied it with the remains of the Flood [18].

Buckland had a brilliant pupil called Charles Lyell, who, after he went down from Oxford, became the first Professor of Geology in the new University of London, at King's College. Between 1830 and 1833 Lyell produced one of the great works in the history of geology, his *Principles of Geology;* this work was said by Charles Darwin to have been one of the most formative influences on the development of his own thought. Here Lyell set out clearly and convincingly the doctrine of uniformitarianism— no wonders, no miracles, no floods—as it had been previously set out by Hutton and Strata Smith. As people moved towards this new geology they were able to appreciate more fully the evidence relating to early man that was coming in.

12. Charles Darwin

It was now coming in from the north of France where a customs official at Abbeville, called Jacques Boucher de Perthes, had been collecting stone implements for a very long time, from the gravels at Abbeville and Amiens. He first thought these were Celtic, and then changed his mind and thought they were pre-Flood. Finally he came to think of them as prehistoric in the sense that we use this word. Two English scholars—antiquaries and geologists—travelled across to see his finds at Abbeville, and were convinced by their authenticity. The first man was Evans, John Evans, an archaeologist, and the second was Prestwich, a geologist. They came back to London certain that what they had seen was direct proof of the great antiquity of man—that there was no doubt about the authenticity of these ancient stone tools made by early man.

The same evidence was being accumulated in south Devon. A schoolmaster in Torquay, by name William Pengelly, excavated first in Kent's Cavern at Torquay and then across the harbour at Brixham. Kent's Cavern was one of the sites with which Dean Buckland had been concerned. It had been suggested to him that here was evidence that the remains of man were found in an

11. Boucher de Perthes

undisturbed level together with remains of extinct animals, and the whole level sealed by a thick level of stalagmite. Buckland never visited this site but told the excavator that he must be wrong: he wrote to the excavator, a Roman Catholic priest called MacEnery, that what he thought he had found must be due to the camping sites of ancient Britons, whose materials had got down through the stalagmite to apparently undisturbed levels. MacEnery wrote back that there was no evidence whatsoever of this, and Buckland replied "Go on looking, you will find it."

Pengelly, who took over from MacEnery, realised at once that he had to work in an undisturbed site, and he found this across the harbour, and began to excavate it in the 1850s at the same time as Boucher de Perthes was working in France. The results were similar. When Pengelley was challenged he said, "The scientific world told us that our statements were impossible. We simply responded with the remark that we had not said that they were possible, only that they were true."

John Evans himself, when he went across to

14. William Pengelly

13. Sir John Evans

see Boucher de Perthes and his finds at Abbeville and Amiens, was dubious and unhappy about this evidence for the great antiquity of man. "Think of their finding flint axes and arrowheads at Abbeville and Amiens, in conjunction with the bones of elephants and rhinoceroses 40 feet below the surface in a bed of drift . . . And then in this cave in Devonshire"—here John Evans was referring to the cave which Pengelly was digging—"they say they have found arrowheads among the bones, the same as reported elsewhere. I can hardly believe it. It will make my Ancient Britons seem quite modern, if man is carried back to the time when, in England, elephants, rhinoceroses, hippopotamuses and tigers were also the inhabitants of this country." But, next day, the hardly credible was demonstrated at Abbeville to be true. And that day, John Evans wrote in his diary, "The flint axes and implements found in the gravel were evidently deposited and disposed at the same time with them. In fact they are the remains of a race of men who existed at the time when the Deluge—or whatever it was—caused these gravel beds to take place." So you see, John Evans was still toying with the idea of the Flood. But Prestwich on the other hand had no doubts, and in May 1859 he addressed the Royal Society on this matter. The title of his paper is interesting. It is called "On the occurrence of flint implements associated with the remains of extinct species in beds of a late geological period at Abbeville and Amiens, and" note this—"at Hoxne, in England." So you see that the flint implements that John Frere had sent to the Society of Antiquaries in 1797 had not, in the end, been forgotten [*19*].

The year 1859 is often described as one of the great years in the history of science—the *annus mirabilis* of nineteenth-century science. The first reason for this was the acceptance of the great antiquity of man. A few years ago, the late Abbé

Breuil, when he gave the Huxley lecture to the Royal Anthropological Institute, said that the discovery of fossil man as contemporary with the big extinct animals then took its place among the triumphs of the human mind. This great discovery was communicated to the Royal Society and the Society of Antiquaries in May of 1859; in November of the same year Charles Darwin published his *The Origin of Species*. This book provided, among many other things, a theory of the organic evolution of man. Archaeology had been providing the evidence for the cultural evolution of man, by studying stones and bronze objects and suggesting that there were certain ages in man's past. Two years before 1859 there had been found at Neanderthal the remains of a primitive type of man. So here were three things happening—the evolution of implements which was archaeology, the finding of Neanderthal man which was human anatomy and palaeontology,

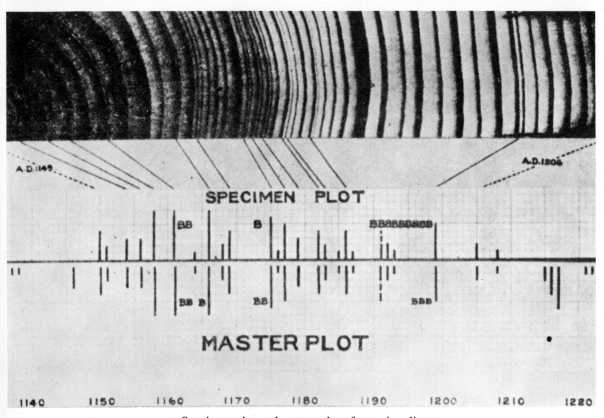

15. Specimen plot and master plot of tree ring diagrams

27

and the theory of Evolution which was biology.

A new climate of thought began to spread from the sixties onwards, but what it did not do was to give an absolute date, even though the antiquity of man was now accepted. From then until the end of the nineteenth century various dates were suggested like 30,000 years, 100,000 years, 200,000 years for the antiquity of man—but these were guesswork—guesses made by the people best qualified to make the guesses, but still guesswork. What was needed was some scientific way to find out early dates—dates that could perhaps be obtained from nature itself. The first of these new techniques was *dendrochronology*, based on

the growth rings in trees. By studying the variation in growth patterns it was possible in America to take back American prehistory from the time of Columbus to the birth of Christ— and this was a beginning. Then in Sweden the Baron de Geer developed a technique of counting clay varves—the thin layers laid down each year by the melt waters of the retreating glaciers of the Great Pleistocene Ice Age. He was able to count these deposits right across Europe and tie them to a known historical moment. His calculations suggested that the last Ice Age came to an end 18,000 years ago. This technique of clay varve counting to which De Geer gave the name *geochronology* was a very important one, and it

16. Professor Willard F. Libby demonstrating part of the equipment for C14 dating

was possible to extend its usefulness by the study of pollen grains. These are practically indestructible and found in various archaeological levels, so that it has been possible to construct from the relationship of the pollen grains to the clay varves the absolute chronology of various types of tree in the post-glacial period [20].

But the most important technique of this kind developed is that of *Carbon 14 dating;* discovered as a by-product of research in nuclear physics in 1945 by Professor Willard F. Libby, at that time Professor of Physics at Chicago—he was awarded the Nobel Prize for his work two years ago. Libby found that all living substances included not only ordinary carbon, Carbon 12, but a radioactive carbon, Carbon 14, which disintegrated at a fixed rate following the death of the living body —plant or animal. It was possible to work out this rate of disappearance: half of it gone in 5,568 years—the so-called half life, and only a quarter would be left in 11,400 years. This means that when you find wood or bones in ancient sites, and if the quantity of C14 to C12 in the specimens is half, then it was approximately 5,500 years ago, i.e. roughly 3500 years B.C., when the wood was burnt or the bones deposited.

This discovery of radiocarbon dating has produced a complete revolution in archaeology. We now have dates for the Palaeolithic and dates for early cultures in Australia and other regions including America, and it has enabled us, by dating accurately the end of the Ice Age, to think back along the curves of the fluctuations of the Ice Age and suggest dates between 600,000 and a million years for the first men. So that man has not only discovered his past, he has produced a complex dating of it. Without trying to say anything about the philosophical implications of the new prehistory, I only want to suggest now that it would be a bold person indeed who said today, as Sir Thomas Browne said in the seventeenth century, "Time we may comprehend: 'tis but five dayes elder than our selves, and hath the same Horoscope with the world." I don't think we yet know what new horoscope of the world prehistoric research has provided for us [21].

III. Lost Civilisations

History, that is to say the written history of the ancient world, has always known of the great Empires—Greece and Rome, the Babylonians, the Medes, the Persians, the Assyrians, and of course Egypt. But it is only archaeology, and archaeology in the last one hundred and fifty years that has revealed to us the first civilisations that existed before those of the ancient world of history.

We begin with Egypt itself; the discovery of ancient man by modern man really dates from the time of Napoleon the First's expedition to that country. He had already a team of artists and scientists working with him in Italy, and when in 1798 he went to Egypt he took with him an even larger team of artists, scientists, and archaeologists—their job was to describe everything they found in Egypt. Of course the obvious monuments of the past, like the Pyramids and the Sphinx were there for all to see: it is reported that before the so-called Battle of the Nile Napoleon mustered his men and said "Soldiers, forty centuries of history look down on you" [22].

However that may be, his scientists, artists and archaeologists started the French Institute in Cairo, and even after Napoleon had been defeated, and Nelson had destroyed the French Fleet in the Battle of Aboukir Bay, the Institute went on. The *Description de l'Egypte* which they produced between 1809 and 1813 is a remarkable work, dealing with the natural history and culture and antiquities of Egypt. The Institute did not engage in any excavation, but it did record portable finds—artifacts found by accident, and of course the surface monuments.

One of the most exciting artifacts found was the Rosetta Stone. This was discovered in 1799 in the excavations—military excavations—by French soldiers of a fort near Alexandria. When, in 1801, the French were forced to evacuate Egypt, the finds that they had hoped would go to the Louvre in Paris, went instead to the British Museum in Bloomsbury; that is why the Rosetta Stone is there for us all to see today [23].

The great importance of the Rosetta Stone is that it has a trilingual inscription—in Greek which could be read, in Demotic Egyptian, the cursive late form of Egyptian writing, and, most important of all, in hieroglyphics—the pictographic writing of early Egypt. This could not be read until the Rosetta Stone was discovered and deciphered. This trilingual inscription was studied by many people, Akerblad in Sweden, Thomas Young in England—there is actually a small part of it translated in an early edition of the *Encyclopedia Britannica*, but the main credit for the decipherment goes very properly to a young French scholar, Jean François Champollion, of the University of Grenoble, who published his translation in 1822. This translation was the key to hieroglyphs, and as a result the key to the ancient history and eventually the prehistory of Egypt [24].

In Mesopotamia work had started even before Egypt. Curiously enough it started with an expedition sent out by the King of Denmark and the Danish Royal Academy under Karsten Nebuhr—Nebuhr was himself a physicist. In Persepolis he and his staff made copies of the writing that was then known for the first time in this area and called *cuneiform* writing because of the wedge-shape of its characters. Nebuhr's party brought back copies of this writing and people began to decipher it. Here is a very salutary lesson, both for the research worker and the teacher. It was a young man, a young German

17. The Rosetta Stone

18. Sir Leonard Woolley

called Grotefend who, in 1802, had taken the first steps towards the decipherment of cuneiform writing. He put up his scheme in a Ph.D thesis to the University of Göttingen, but the Academy there declined it, saying that he was not an oriental scholar, but an ordinary schoolmaster—as he was. As a result Grotefend's work was not published until 1893; by that time others had deciphered cuneiform and received the credit for doing so.

The man who had the main credit was Henry Creswicke Rawlinson; in Persia he had made a special study of the inscription put up by command of Darius the First in 516 B.C. on the great rock of Behistun. This was cut on the rock face 400 feet above ground, and the footholds of the sculptors were then taken away, for Darius intended that the inscription should never be defaced. Rawlinson had great difficulty in recording the inscription; he did most of it him-

self, and could find no one to help him until, as he said, he was assisted by "a wild Kurdish boy who had come from a distance." This boy was very brave and agile; he somehow fastened himself to the rock face with his toes and his hands, and eventually built a construction across, and with a sort of painter's cradle was able to take paper squeezes of the inscriptions. And so the Darius inscriptions were available for study, in London and elsewhere. This was also a trilingual inscription—in Old Persian, Babylonian and Elamite. Now as the decipherment of cuneiform took place, some scholars said that it was a form of writing that must have been devised by pre-Semitic people, and even went so far as to suggest that these were the Sumerians who lived in Mesopotamia in the time before the Babylonians and Assyrians. A little later, the French Consul at Basra, de Sarzec, began digging at a place nearby called Telloh and here he unearthed a remarkable series of statues, like that of the Governor of the City, Gudea, now in the Louvre. De Sarzec worked on until 1900 and by then had revealed clearly the Sumerians, the pre-Semitic people who had invented cuneiform writing.

Perhaps the Sumerians are best known to us from the work of Sir Leonard Woolley in the 1920s, work which culminated in the discovery of the Royal Tombs at Ur in 1926. A few years before in the Valley of the Tombs, Howard Carter and Lord Caernarvon, after years of patient prospecting, had unearthed Tutankamen's tomb. This was one of the greatest finds—the richest finds—ever made, and I can remember as a small boy the excitement caused by the discovery in the years following 1922. The finds, or most of them, were taken to the Museum in Cairo where at the present day they make a magnificent display. 1926 is another memorable year in man's discovery of his past, for by then some of his lost civilisations had been recovered [25].

The Bronze Age civilisations of the Eastern Mediterranean, the lost civilisations that lay behind classical Greece, were discovered by two archaeologists, the one a German, Heinrich Schliemann, and the other an Englishman, Arthur

19. The Rock of Behistun

Evans. They came from very different backgrounds. Schliemann was the son of a poor pastor in Germany and was brought up with no wealth and little excitement. One year his father gave him a copy of Jerrer's *Universal History* for a Christmas present. There he saw a drawing of Troy in flames and this fired his youthful imagination; at the time—a young boy of eight—he said "One day I shall find Troy." This seemed a childish ambition and a childish boast, but it happened. This was the great excitement of Schliemann's career. His was a strange life full of adventure but he quickly established himself as a business man. He made a fortune in Russia, another in America and in the 1850s retired at the age of 46—this successful merchant banker and business man—to devote himself to archaeology. In 1871 he travelled around in the Aegean and Western

Anatolia and started excavations at one site, that of Hissarlik. He cut a great section through the mound and of it wrote "There was and is at the site of Troy no sublimer place than this." He referred to it as the Tower of Ilium and all the time in his excavations he was relating what he found to Homer. He was very fortunate in his excavation and found among other things a rich treasure, which he called the Treasure of Priam; this is nothing to do with Priam, but is a treasure of the Bronze Age of the second millennium B.C.

In the intervals of his four seasons of work at Troy, Schliemann dug on the mainland of Greece, at sites like Mycenae and Tiryns and Orchomenos. At Troy he knew what he was looking for—he dug at Hissarlik because he was looking for the old Troy, the old Ilium of legend and saga. He did not quite know what he was looking for on

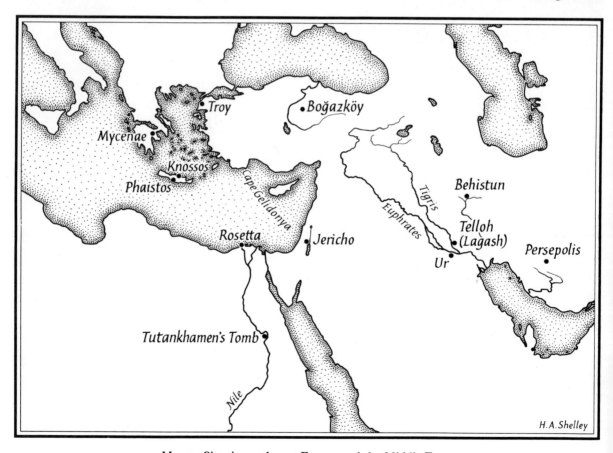

Map 2. Sites in south-east Europe and the Middle East

20. Gold and Lapis Lazuli mask of the Pharaoh Tutankhamen

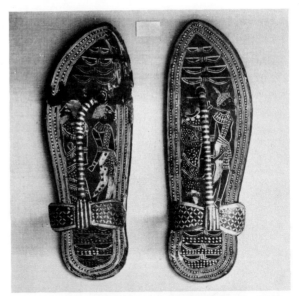

21. Decorated sandals from Tutankhamen's tomb

the mainland of Greece and he was surprised when he found the remains of another rich Bronze Age civilisation, the civilisation of the mainland of Europe, perhaps one might call it the first European civilisation; he called it the Mycenean civilisation from the great site of Mycenae. Schliemann's most exciting finds were made in the shaft graves inside the citadel of Mycenae; here was a mass of gold work. No one going into the National Museum at Athens can come away without a sense of surprise and wonder and excitement at the richness and magnificence of the gold work from Mycenae. Schliemann thought he was still dealing with Homer and called one of the richest gold masks the Mask of Agamemnon [26].

Schliemann had found this surprising lost civilisation. How did it start? Where did it come from? and for that matter what lay behind the

Bronze Age civilisation of Troy? Not, at least directly, Egypt, but perhaps somewhere between Egypt and Greece. Those interested in this problem had begun to look south from Greece, and south from Greece was Crete.

From Crete there had been found seals with curious markings on them. Schliemann himself thought of excavating in Crete, but died before he could manage this. It was an Englishman, Arthur Evans, who excavated in Crete and discovered its lost civilisation. Arthur Evans was the son of Sir John Evans, whom we have already talked about in connexion with the discovery of ancient man at Abbeville and Amiens; and Arthur Evans, like his father, started with an interest in European archaeology. He became Keeper of the Ashmolean Museum in Oxford, and his interests moved to the archaeology of the East Mediterranean. In 1899 he started excavating at Knossos in Crete, and within nine weeks had revealed the remains of a large and remarkable palace. He went on excavating there and at other sites, and called the lost civilisation he had newly discovered the Minoan; some thought that was a strange thing to do as Minos was the destroyer not the creator of the civilisation of Crete—but however that may be, the name Minoan was adopted. The

22. Heinrich Schliemann

23. Sophie Schliemann, wearing jewels found on the site of Troy

art of the Minoan civilisation was one of its most remarkable features, with a character entirely of its own, and unlike that of Egypt and Sumeria. The Bull Cult of the Minoans is one of the most interesting aspects of the civilisation, and so are the figures and dresses of the women—almost like something from Parisian *haute couture* [27].

Arthur Evans found in Crete three kinds of writing. The first was pictographic as shown by the Phaestos Disc from another palace site. The second and third were not pictographic but linear forms of writing, which Evans labelled Linear A and Linear B. Linear A has not yet been deciphered, but Linear B was deciphered recently by the late Michael Ventris and John Chadwick. Ventris gave the first news of this decipherment in a broadcast on the B.B.C. Third Programme, published in *The Listener* in 1953 [28].

While Schliemann was working at Troy,

another civilisation was being discovered to the east, the civilisation of the Hittites. In 1860 a French art historian named Perrot visited the large ruined city of Boğasköy, east of Ankara, in Central Anatolia, and realised he was looking at an entirely new art. Later Professor Sayce of Oxford put together all that was then known about this civilisation and defined it as the civilisation of the Hittites. A German expedition under Hugo Winckler dug at Boğasköy and found a large quantity of cuneiform tablets. Still later a Czech named Hrozny was able to decipher them, and to show that one of the languages spoken by the Hittites was an Indo-European language. So yet a fourth great east Mediterranean prehistoric civilisation had been discovered by archaeology, and found by a combination of archaeologists from various countries; this is not surprising since archaeology, like man himself, is an international affair [29].

24. View of the main excavation area dug by
Schliemann at Troy

25. Portrait of Sir Arthur Evans

26. Knossos—view of the Palace and the surrounding country from the east

In the half-century, then, between 1850 and 1900 the archaeologist with his spade had discovered in south-west Asia five lost civilisations—that of the Sumerians in Mesopotamia, those of the Hittites and Trojans in Anatolia, that of the Myceneans in mainland Greece, and that of the Minoans in Crete. Scholars began to wonder about the old world further east, the world of India and China, which had certainly been in contact with Greece and Rome and which some people thought must have supported old civilisations. Was there in these areas anything older than the ancient historic civilisations, anything comparable with the Bronze Age civilisations discovered in the Mediterranean and south-west Asia? In 1922, the Director of Archaeology in

India, Sir John Marshall, was complaining that there was no such evidence of prehistoric civilisation in that country. In the first volume of the *Cambridge History of India*, published in that year, Marshall wrote "It is the misfortune of Indian history that its earliest and most obscure pages are able to derive little light from contemporary antiquities'. Yet, two years later, in the pages of *The Illustrated London News*, he was announcing that members of his staff excavating in two large mounds in what is now Pakistan—the sites of Mohenjo-daro and Harappa in the Indus Valley—had discovered a prehistoric civilisation which he compared at once with the early civilisation of Sumeria; he declared that these discoveries were comparable in importance with

27. Knossos—the Hall of the Double Axes in the Palace of Minos

28. Storage room in the Palace of Knossos—bull symbol in the middle distance

29. Example of Linear B writing

the discoveries made by Schliemann in Troy and Mycenae—and he was quite right.

This civilisation, now usually referred to as the Indus or Harappan civilisation, is still best seen from the two first found sites—Mohenjo-daro and Harappa. These cities both have one remarkable feature, their streets are laid out in a criss-cross or grid pattern. With its brick walls and brick drains and straight main streets Mohenjo-daro is a remarkable city—the first example of city planning in the history of man. An interesting feature of the Indus or Harappan civilisation is its seals—they have on them animals and writing, writing which has not developed beyond picture writing. This writing has not been deciphered, but even if it were it would not unlock a great literature as the decipherment of Sumerian has. It would presumably produce for us no more than lists of kings and priests and commodities and perhaps places.

The Indus civilisation, which dates from the third and second millennia B.C. has been studied afresh at the end of the last war and since. Sir Mortimer Wheeler was appointed Director of Archaeology in India in 1944 and among his tasks paid special attention to the Indus cities with their ceremonial baths around which were houses for priests—a feature of Indian life which as many will know, survives to the present day, sacred tanks being found in many villages and cities of today. While Mohenjo-daro and Harappa remain extremely important sites, modern research has extended the range of the Indus civilisation down to Bombay and up to Delhi; and in the last few years a port has been found, at Lothal, from which we can envisage the Indus traders sailing along the coast of Persia and up the Persian gulf to the cities of Sumeria. There certainly was contact between these old civilisations of Mesopotamia and India [30].

30. Ruins at Mohenjo-daro

31. Indus Valley seal

Was there contact still further east, to China? Here we must talk about the city of Anyang. During the last few decades of the nineteenth century, farmers tilling their fields at a little village near Anyang right in the north of China, came across curious pieces of bone, some decorated with characters. These are generally referred to as Oracle Bones, and this is how they were used. Their use was a form of augury which has survived to the present day in certain Mongol tribes and consists of applying a heated metal point to one side of the shoulder blade of an animal or to the shell of a tortoise. This produces cracks on the other side, often running approximately at right-angles to each other, and the interpretation of these cracks answers the questions which were put to the oracle. In 1928, because of the finding of many of these oracle

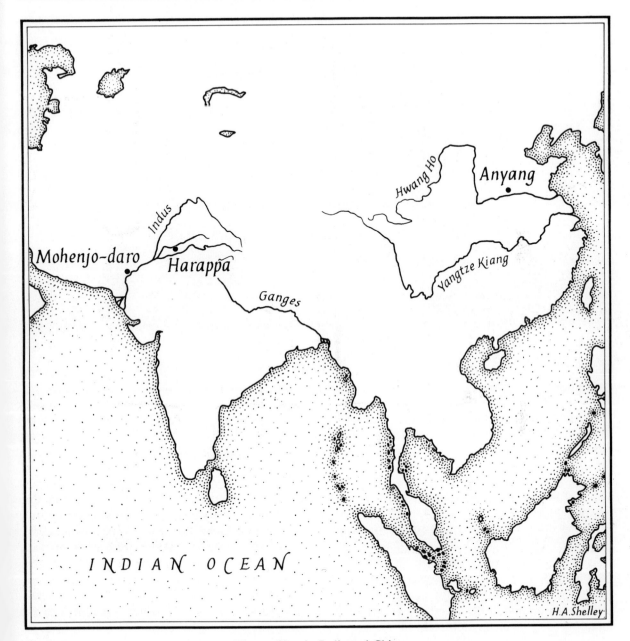

Map 3. Sites in India and China

bones at Anyang, the Chinese Academy, together with the Smithsonian Institution in America, made a series of excavations at Anyang; they revealed a Bronze Age city, and found an ancient Bronze Age Chinese civilisation. This work was carried on after the war by the present Chinese Government, who have organised a great deal of research into this problem, and now no less than one hundred and twenty five Anyang-type sites have been found dating from the second millennium B.C. This is later than the Sumerian cities, and later than the Indus and Egyptian cities—

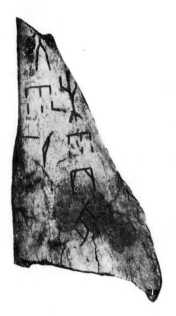

32. Oracle bones from Anyang, China

more comparable in time with the Minoan civilisation. It has been possible to equate the civilisation of Anyang found by the spade with the Shang dynasty of historical China. We know that the Shang kings paid a great deal of attention to oracle bones; there was one who consulted the oracle practically every day—on one occasion we find him asking why he had toothache and which of his ancestors was responsible for giving it to him [31].

So far we have been talking about the Old World. There were also lost civilisations in the New World waiting for the archaeologists. In the late fifteenth and early sixteenth century when the *conquistadores*, the Spanish and Portuguese conquerors of middle America got there, they found three living civilisations, that of the Aztecs of Mexico, the Mayas of Yucatan, Honduras and Guatemala, and the Incas of Peru. They virtually destroyed these three civilisations, hitherto unknown to the old world, and no one paid much attention to what the Aztecs, Mayas and Incas had achieved. Columbus had anyway been looking for the Indies; in discovering America he and his followers had virtually walked back into pre-

history and found themselves in the equivalent of the Bronze Age civilisations of Sumeria, Egypt and Crete. It was as though when going to Mexico City they had gone to Ur or Mohenjo-daro or Harappa. But no one paid much attention, as I have said, to these and other early American civilisations until the nineteenth century.

One may say that American archaeology began in 1842 when the American, Stephens, and the English draughtsman, Catherwood, went and visited remains of idols and temples like Copán in Yucatan, and the Mayas were rediscovered. Then, scholars began to take an interest in the American past. In the last thirty to forty years intense work has been done on the lost civilisations of America by research organisations in America, Mexico, and Peru. These discoveries in America, and the discovery of the lost civilisations of the old world, do not only mean that the archaeologist was discovering his civilised past. He has posed by the spade a problem of how to explain the past and asked two questions: how did civilisation come into existence, and what were the inter-relations of these early civilisations in the Old and New Worlds [32].

IV. From Savagery to Civilisation

In 1865 when Sir John Lubbock wrote his *Prehistoric Times* he distinguished, as I have said, between two Stone Ages, the Old Stone Age or Palaeolithic, and the New Stone Age or Neolithic. Because of Carbon 14 dating we now know that the Neolithic—the time of the first peasant farmers —began in Europe, or parts of Europe as early as the sixth millennium B.C. Before say 6000 B.C. Europe was in the Old Stone Age, or the Palaeo-lithic and Mesolithic as later defined. The Old Stone Age was at first characterised by coarsely chipped flint implements—the sort of things found at Abbeville and Amiens and by John Frere at Hoxne. But in the south of France a different kind of Palaeolithic was being discovered—the Old Stone Age of people who lived in rock shelters in south-western France—the Dordogne area—and the Pyrenees. The person who first worked extensively on these matters was Edouard Lartet, who gave up his legal practice to devote himself to the study of palaeontology and arch-aeology. He worked first in the Pyrenees, finding in cave shelters not only flint implements but decorated objects of bone. While he was working in the Pyrenees he was sent a box of flint imple-ments from an area that has since been referred to as the capital of prehistory in France, the region around Les Eyzies where the rivers Dordogne and Vézère meet. So he went to work there and was assisted in his work by the English banker and hat-maker Henry Christy. They worked in rock-shelters like La Madeleine and Le Moustier, and many other sites which have since become household words in French arch-aeology. And as they worked in these rock-shelters they went on finding decorated objects —spear-throwers and the like, and engravings on flat pebbles and pieces of stone.

It was not only decorated objects and pieces of stone that began to appear in these contexts but figurines of females—females with certain aspects of their figures exaggerated: perhaps they were fertility figures. The so-called Venus of Bras-sempouy is a good example; it comes almost from the Atlantic coast of France. These female figurines occur right across Europe and into Russia. There clearly existed among the hunters and fishers of the later part of the Old Stone Age a fertility cult.

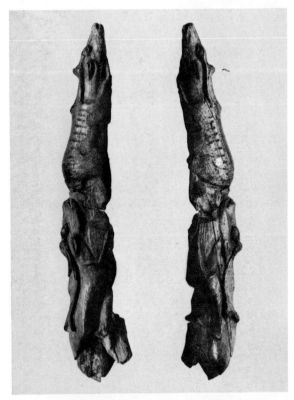

33. Decorated spear-throwers from a Rock-Shelter, Bruniquel, now in the British Museum

34. Venus of Brassempouy

The art of the decorated spear-throwers and the female figurines was obvious; its existence could not be denied. The hunter-fishers of the end of the Old Stone Age, of 30,000 to 10,000 years ago were our first artists. But in 1875 there was a challenge, and scholars began to wonder whether in fact these Old Stone Age artists did other works of art than spear-throwers and fat ladies. De Sautuola, a Spaniard, had, a few years before, discovered a cave with paintings on the walls, and he excavated there. One day, his

36. Engraved bison on a limestone plaque from Bruniquel

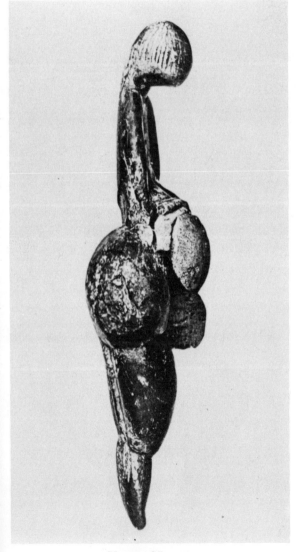

35. Venus of Lespugue

daughter aged five, bored with her father's excavations, wandered into the depth of the cave, which was very low and which her father had not visited because of its inaccessibility. There by the light of her torch she saw on the roof of the inner part of this cave—the now very famous cave of Altamira—vigorous, bold, striking paintings of bulls and bison and charging boars. She went out to tell her father, saying "*Toros, Toros,* father, come and see the bulls!" He went in and saw these remarkable paintings in red and brown and bistre, and told the world about his great discovery [*33*].

Most of the scholarly world did not believe him; it said the paintings were forgeries or done in historical times, and as always happens in these *causes célèbres*, from murders to forgeries, a man came forward and said he had painted the bulls himself. Altamira became a dirty word and was not mentioned at archaeological meetings and conferences for a long time.

Some people, however, believed in Altamira. The Director of the French National Museum of Antiquities declared that Altamira was not a forgery, nor modern, nor the work of a child. He

37. Party of scientists at La Mouthe: the young Henri Breuil is 4th from right

said "Here we have the infancy of art." In the last few years of the nineteenth century other sites were found which proved the authenticity of Altamira and of cave art in general. The most important site was La Mouthe near Les Eyzies; here wall paintings in the depths of the cave were found only after digging through Palaeolithic deposits completely masking the entrance to the inner part of the cave. After a scientific conference at Montauban a party went up to look at La Mouthe and realised that the evidence presented there was indisputable. Two of the party— Cartailhac who was Professor at Toulouse, and a young protégé of his who was to become the most famous worker in Palaeolithic archaeology, the Abbé Henri Breuil—went off to visit Altamira

38. Bison, Altamira

and realised that the scepticism of the scholarly archaeological world about this site was misplaced. From now on Altamira and La Mouthe were authentic and prehistoric cave art was a fact of man's remote past.

From then on until the present day the story has been one of the steady and gradual discovery of more examples of this most ancient wall art of man. The most exciting discovery was made on the 12th September, 1940 at Lascaux. It was made by four boys who were out rabbiting with their dog Robot. The dog fell down through a hole in the roof of the cave—a hole made by the uprooting of a tree in the previous winter's gales.

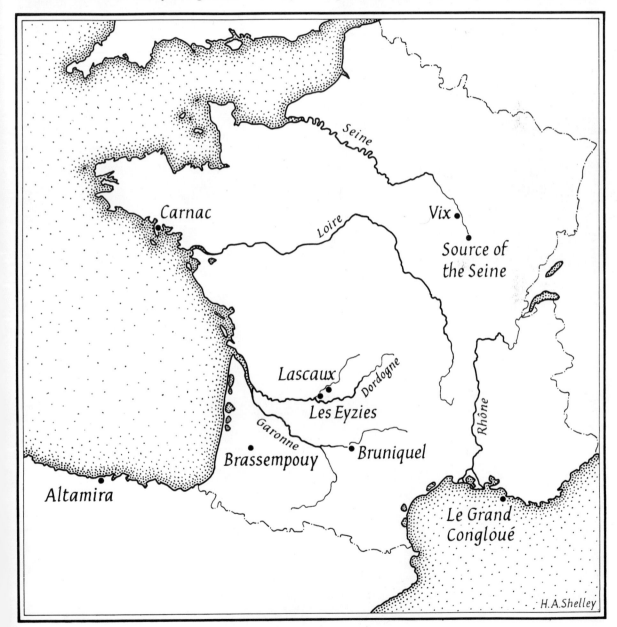

Map 4. Sites in France and Spain

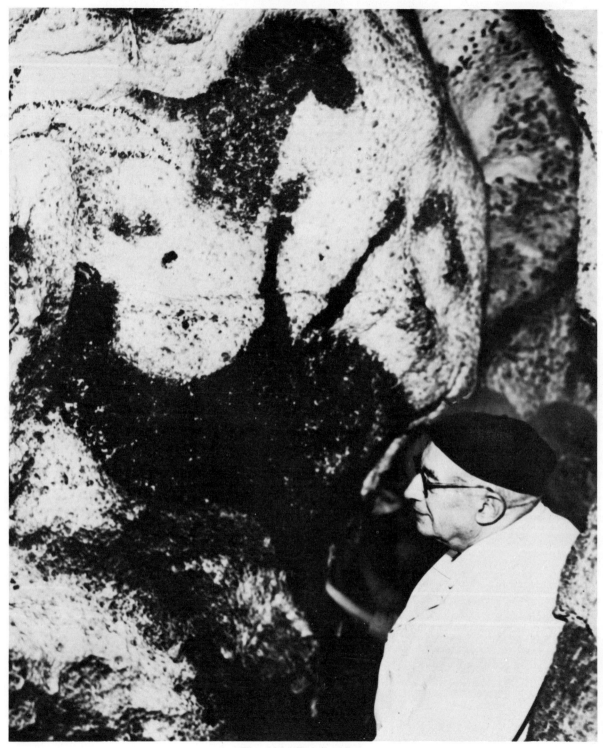

39. The Abbé Breuil at Lascaux

40. The scene from Lascaux

The boys climbed down to rescue their dog, and found themselves in a large cave the walls and roof of which were decorated with painted and engraved animals. Altamira and Lascaux are not art galleries, they are probably sacred or special sites where some form of sympathetic hunting magic was performed.

There are very few scenes in this very old cave art, but one such does occur in a very inaccessible place at Lascaux. The scene shows a wounded bison—his innards are tumbling out, his head is turned round in not unnatural surprise, and perhaps the hunter—very badly drawn as were all human beings in Palaeolithic art—is shown in front of the dying animal, and then a spear-thrower, and a bird on a stick. We cannot explain this scene, and my purpose here is just to draw attention to it and to the fact that between 1875 and 1940 Palaeolithic cave art was discovered as a part of man's past. There is a sad footnote to

all this: in the last few years it was discovered that some of the Palaeolithic cave-paintings were fading and that at Lascaux they were being covered with a fungus. This decay has now been checked at Lascaux but it appears that the fading is going on elsewhere. It would be sad if man, having discovered in the last century his oldest art, was now unable to keep it intact, and ready to be seen by the millions who are now interested in prehistory. There must be some way in which it is possible to preserve for us intact the oldest art of savage Europe [34].

I deliberately said "savage Europe," and it may seem strange to us that the people who painted so well and with such assurance at Altamira and Lascaux and La Mouthe should be called savages, but that is what they were in the technical sense. They did not know anything about the domestication of animals and about agriculture. I suggest this is the way to think about them: after man—

49

homo sapiens—had been in existence for a long time and towards the end of his life as a hunter, a fisher, and a food-gatherer, at a time which radio-carbon dating would put at between 30,000 and 10,000 B.C., he had achieved some very remarkable arts and crafts, including the art displayed in portable objects and on the walls of sacred caves. All this showed where you could get to in the development of savagery, without sudden and remarkable change.

Then came the great change, perhaps the greatest change in human history, which the late Professor Gordon Childe called "the Neolithic Revolution." Because it is such a great change, and of such fundamental importance in human history, the work of the archaeologist who traces the origins of this change—where it happened, how it happened, when it happened, and for that matter, how often it happened—is of fundamental importance to our understanding of human history [*35*].

Food gathering and food production are the two great stages in human history, but what is interesting is that food production did not follow on from the brilliant artists, the food gatherers of southern France and northern Spain. There were in any case no wild crops or animals suitable for domestication in those areas. The first domestication of crops and animals occurred in what is often described as the most ancient Near East,

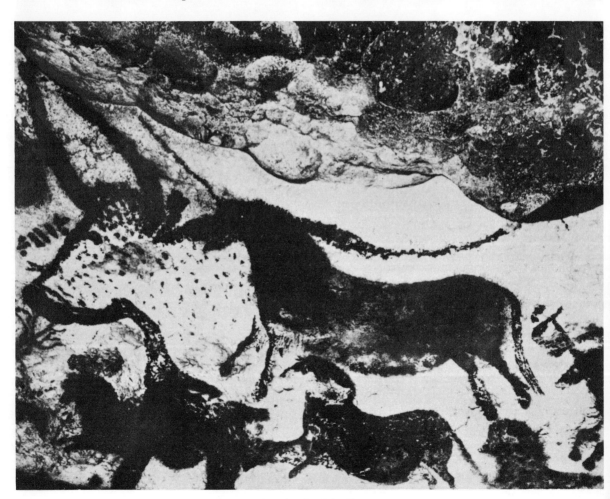

41. Painted animals at Lascaux

and the Near East that is more ancient than the civilisations we have already been talking about—the civilisations of Sumeria and Egypt. It used to be said twenty or thirty years ago—and this is the great change that has taken place in our knowledge of man's past—that agriculture and domesticated animals started in Egypt and Mesopotamia on the horns of what Breasted called the Fertile Crescent between Cairo and Basra [36].

We know now that this is not so, and that these fundamental discoveries were made in the north of Mesopotamia—in the foothills of the Zagros Mountains, where American excavators have been working; in Palestine, where Dr Kathleen Kenyon has been working in Jericho; and in

southern Anatolia, where people like James Mellaart have been working. So the picture we now have of man's discovery of food production—I deliberately say his first discovery because it is possible that separate similar discoveries were made in India and in China, and certain that similar discoveries were made in America—is of discovery in Palestine, north Mesopotamia and southern Anatolia, in that triangle (not a crescent) of the Near East [37].

Let us take Jericho as an example. This fine tell or mound of accumulated deposits was dug by Dr Kathleen Kenyon between 1952 and 1958 and her discovery of what happened in ancient Jericho is one of the most important new dis-

42. Jericho—general view

coveries of man's past made in the last quarter-century. She was able to get right down to the beginnings of settlement at Jericho, and to find a food-producing settlement nearly ten thousand years ago. Since the Jericho excavations a series of digs has revealed the spread of the earliest arts of agriculture to Europe for example, a study in which American, Greek, British, Bulgarian, Russian, Yugoslav and other archaeologists have taken part. We know that the first peasant farmers—the first Neolithic people—did not arrive in southern Britain until round about 3500 B.C. [38].

The spread of peasant village agriculture is one aspect of the change from the savagery of the Old Stone Age to the barbarism of the New Stone Age. Archaeology has had much light to throw on the life of the barbarian societies who lived in the twilight of history half way between the savage artists of Altamira and the civilisations of Egypt and Sumer—the people of the high barbarian cultures, as American archaeologists call them. I choose as an example the people who built the great megalithic monuments of western Europe. We have some particularly fine examples of these monuments in the British Isles. New Grange is one—a great circular mound 250 feet in diameter and 30 feet in height, not too far from Dublin—indeed between Dublin and Drogheda, ten miles west of Drogheda. Inside this great mound is a finely built prehistoric stone tomb which was discovered for the first time in the late seventeenth century. It is only in the last quarter century that comparative study of similar tombs in Brittany

43. New Grange—aerial view

and Spain and Portugal have shown us that the barbarian builders of New Grange probably moved up the Atlantic seaways from Iberia [*39*].

In southern Britain we have a different kind of megalithic tomb: West Kennet, recently excavated by Professor Piggott and Professor Atkinson, is one of this kind. This tomb is different in plan from New Grange and represents a separate tradition of megalith tomb-building which perhaps developed not on the Atlantic seaways, but in northern France and Britain itself [*40*]. The stone circles of the British Isles are in some ways even more intriguing than the megalithic tombs. We have already spoken of Stonehenge several times; it has been visible to the general public for centuries, and for centuries was attributed to the Druids. Antiquaries like Colt Hoare and Cunnington might well wonder whether any fresh answer other than Druids could be obtained for this remarkable monument. Yet that fresh answer has been obtained by archaeologists digging in the last fifteen years; they were able to show that Stonehenge was a monument constructed between 2000 and 1400 B.C., a prehistoric cathedral with several periods of construction. In the last period, the period of Stonehenge III, many of us think there must have been a Mycenean architect at work, or rather someone who knew of the Mycenean structures which Schliemann and others after him had found. This is not only because of the technique of architecture, but because of contemporary British objects found in Mycenae and Mycenean objects found in Britain. There is a Mycenean dagger from Cornwall and on one of the stones of Stonehenge itself the recently discovered engraving of a possibly Mycenean dagger [*41*]. I make this point because we must always remember that the illiterate barbarian societies of prehistoric Europe were always in some kind of contact with the literate civilisations of south-eastern Europe and the east Mediterranean [*42*].

It was prehistoric archaeology that discovered the contacts between Mycenae and Salisbury Plain, but it had been known from ancient history itself that there was contact between the literate civilisations of Greece, Etruria and Rome and the people who lived on the fringes of the classical world, the people whom the Greeks called barbarians—those who could not speak Greek, and went *ba-ba*. The Greeks knew the names of some of these people or tribes—the Sarmatians, Scythians, Ligurians, Celts. It was the Celts or Gauls that the Greeks and Romans mainly described when they were talking about European barbarians and they admittedly had only a rather shadowy picture of them, a picture occasionally made sharper and clearer when the Gauls sacked Rome in 390 B.C. and Alexander received a deputation of Celts in 335 B.C.

But the picture of the Celts and Gauls from ancient history is still vague and shadowy—one full of warriors and Druids—barbarians in the real sense of the word, meaning people who were not cultivated, not civilised. It is archaeology which has shown that these people were near cultivated, near civilised. The Celts lived in towns and in great entrenched enclosures, or hill-forts, like Maiden Castle—which covers over a hundred acres and whose ramparts still stand up to a height of 60 feet. Standing on the ground looking up at the enormous multi-vallate ramparts of Maiden Castle one begins to sense the organisation that must have existed among the barbarian Celts who built major engineering works of this kind. What we know about Maiden Castle is the result of the excavation in the years immediately before the second world war of this site by Sir Mortimer Wheeler. He was able to unravel a long and complicated history of the site beginning at least two thousand years B.C. in the Neolithic period and going on to the time when this splendid barbarian citadel was slighted by the Romans, and replaced by the Roman town of Dorchester near by [*43*].

The Celts buried their dead in various ways, but their rich and famous were buried in graves with their chariots, carts or hearses. One of the most famous of these is from Somme-Bionne in the Marne area of the North of France. Much of our knowledge of the Celts has been built up from these rich princely burials. The most famous and remarkable of these was found at Vix, north of Dijon as recently as 1953. It is the burial of a

44. Stonehenge from the south

45. Maiden Castle—aerial view

princess with her hearse or cart which may have been in domestic use before her death. She seems to have reigned over a tribe who lived on the main trade route from the Mediterranean to the British Isles—a route that went up the Rhône-Saône valley and over the Morvan hills of north Burgundy to the Seine valley and the English Channel. This rich grave was discovered by Monsieur René Joffroy when a Professor in the Lyceé of Châtillon-sur-Seine; he is now Director General of the French National Museum of Antiquities at St-Germain-en-Laye. One of the

Map 5. Sites in England, Wales and Ireland

most astonishing things in this rich grave was the great bronze *krater*—a vessel nearly six feet in height—the largest vessel of its kind that has survived from antiquity. That an object like this of Greek or Greco-Etruscan workmanship could be traded, probably full of wine, up to the north of Burgundy from its place of manufacture in Greece or Italy gives some indication of the sort of relationship that existed in prehistoric times between Mediterranean civilisation and the European barbarians [*44*].

The discovery of Vix took place in 1953. Ten years later another great find was made at the source of the river Seine between Vix and Dijon. This discovery was made by Professor Martin of the University of Dijon who had been working at this site for some while; in 1963 he discovered nearly 200 wooden objects excellently preserved, many of them heads of men and women, eight to ten or twelve inches in height. It was a remarkable find and the job of preservation has also been remarkable. I went recently to see the site and the figures in the University of Dijon: after

47. The Vix Diadem

preservation the heads look as fresh as though they had been cut out of heart oak only yesterday. They may have formed part of a shrine, or perhaps were the contents of a store where pilgrims bought heads and other objects as presents —*ex-votos*—to the shrine of the goddess Sequana at the source of the Seine. Excavations are to continue there for several years, and many more remarkable objects may be found [*45*].

Rome conquered the Celtic barbarians, but there still remained barbarians outside Rome, and many who outlasted Rome. Among the most colourful and exciting are the Vikings. In 1880 the son of a farmer owning a barrow or tumulus

46. The Gundestrup bowl

48. Tomb of Princess at Vix. Handle of the *Krater*

at Gokstad on the west side of Oslo fjord began to dig, looking for treasure, but found instead a great Viking ship. A quarter of a century later, while he was celebrating his birthday in the National Museum at Oslo, Professor Gustafson was interrupted by a farmer who had come to say that he had found the remains of a ship on his land. This land was at Oseberg, ten miles north of Gokstad, and about thirty miles south of Oslo. Gustafson excavated the ship—a sailing ship 70 feet long. These ships are now in a special museum built for them just outside Oslo.

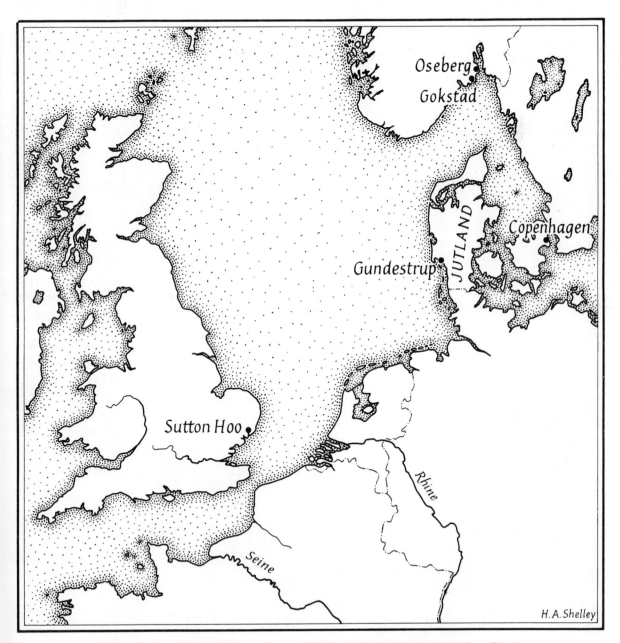

Map 6. Sites of the Iron Age and post Roman period in England and Scandinavia

49. The Gokstad Ship

50. The Oseberg Ship

51. The Sutton Hoo Ship

Just before the outbreak of the 1939–45 war another ship was discovered this time at Sutton Hoo in south-east England. This ship was about the same length as the Gokstad and Oseberg ships, about 70 feet, but it is lighter in construction and dates from the seventh century A.D. perhaps 150 years before the Viking ships of Oslo fjord. The Sutton Hoo ship lay in sand and practically everything perishable had vanished, including the timbers of the ships which could only be identified by the rows of clinch nails that were in position, and the discoloration of the soil itself. In the centre of the ship was a great treasure which had not been reached by tomb robbers. You can see it now in the British Museum where it is one of that great museum's great treasures [46].

I have summarised in this talk a few of the important and spectacular discoveries made by archaeologists studying the savages and barbarians in prehistoric Europe. Many archaeological discoveries in Europe and elsewhere are made by accident; there is still room for luck and the amateur in archaeology. But if the amateur finds anything that he thinks is important he should get in touch with professionals so that the Professor Gustafsons of the world can take over.

V. Science and Modern Archaeology

Most of us associate archaeology with excavation; this is the first activity people think of when you mention archaeology to them, and it is perfectly true that excavation is the essential activity in the archaeological study of man's past. Of course digging is not the be-all and end-all of archaeology, but without excavation man would not have discovered his past. So the development of scientific excavation which took place at the end of the nineteenth century and the beginning of the present century is in a way the key development in the history of archaeology.

There was plenty of excavation before the end of the nineteenth century and sometimes it was very strange work. Antiquarians in England would think nothing of excavating half a dozen round barrows in a day; whereas today the proper excavation of a round barrow can take anything from four to six weeks. And it is no use denying that some of the people working in Egypt, Mesopotamia and Greece were simply tomb-robbers. In the sixteenth century Lord Arundel said, quite frankly, that his purpose was "to transplant old Greece to England," and we find people like Sir Henry Layard himself remarking that the cause of his excavations at Nimrud was "to obtain the largest number of works of art with the least possible outlay of time and money." Robert Wood, who produced a fine book on the ruins of Palmyra, said, "The inscriptions we copied as they fell in our way, and carried off the marbles whenever it was possible, for the avarice and superstition of the inhabitants made the task difficult and sometimes impracticable." The Cambridge don E. D. Clarke recounts how he got the colossal Cistophoros of Eleusis, now in the Fitzwilliam Museum, away from Greece. It is a fascinating story of archaeological method in the early nineteenth century. "I found the Goddess in a dung hill" he wrote, "buried to her ears, and the Eleusinian peasants at the very mention of moving it regarded me as one who would bring the Moon from her orbit. What would become of their corn, they said, if the old lady with the basket were removed. I went to Athens and made an application to the Pasha, aiding my request by letting an English telescope glide through his fingers. The business was soon done" [47].

The most colourful figure in early nineteenth century archaeology was without any doubt Giovanni Belzoni, an Italian who became a naturalised Englishman. We first meet him being a strong man in circuses and operas, then unsuccessfully selling hydraulic machinery in Egypt, then starting on a career of tomb-robbing, providing material for the British Museum by what he called his "operations." Here is an extract from what he says: "When my weight bore on an Egyptian it crushed like a bandbox. I naturally had recourse to my hands to sustain my weight but they found no better support so that I sank altogether among the broken mummies with a crash of bones and rags and wooden cases. Every step I took I crushed a mummy in some part or other. Once I was conducted from such a place to another resembling it through a passage some 20 feet in length and no wider than a body could be forced through. It was choked with mummies and I could not pass it without my face coming into contact with that of some ancient and decayed Egyptian. I could not avoid being covered with legs and arms and heads, all decayed and decaying, which were all rolling on me from above". And then this ingenuous sentence: "the purpose of my researches"—researches, indeed!—"was to rob the Egyptians of their papyri which I found, some hidden in their breasts, under their arms, in the space above their knees, and on the legs" [*48*].

That is not an unfair account of what was going on in the early nineteenth century in Egypt, the Middle East and the east Mediterranean. The pioneers of systematic and scientific excavation were the men who worked in these areas in the second half of the nineteenth century. The Germans at Olympia must be regarded as some of the first and most careful excavators. In this chapter I pay particular attention to two Englishmen, real pioneers of scientific excavation. The first was Sir Flinders Petrie who spent the greater part of his long life working in Egypt. Petrie wrote his *Ten Years Digging in Egypt* in 1892, and his *Methods and Aims in Archaeology* in 1904. He died in 1942, in his 90th year; he called his autobiography *Seventy Years in Archaeology*. Nowadays some of the things he wrote in his *Methods and Aims in Archaeology* read a little oddly. Take this passage: "To attempt serious work in pretty suits, shiny leggings or starched collars, would be like mountaineering in evening dress . . . to suppose that work can be controlled from a distant hotel, where the master lives in

53. Giovanni Belzoni

52. Sir Flinders and Lady Petrie with their archaeological bus

54. General Pitt-Rivers

state and luxury completely out of touch with his men, is a fallacy . . . A telescope is very useful to watch if distant work is regular . . . A telescope will also show if a boy is put up to watch for the master's coming" [49].

The second Englishman was General Pitt-Rivers, who was a regular soldier by name Augustus Lane Fox until in 1880 he inherited great estates on Cranborne Chase in Dorset. One of the requisites of this inheritance was that he change his name to Pitt-Rivers, which he did. From 1880 until his death in 1900, he performed a miracle of archaeological field work, excavation, and recording, all of which he did with military precision, and with an inspired technique that really amounted to genius. He had admittedly plenty of money and time, plenty of workmen, whom he treated rather as though they were his private soldiers—but he got excellent results and established the basis of modern archaeological technique [50].

After the death of Pitt-Rivers in 1900 a few people working in north-western Europe tried to carry out his methods, but very few. The war of 1914–18 put a stop to all archaeological excavation, and during it many promising archaeologists

55. Excavation of a round barrow near Amesbury on Salisbury Plain, by Paul Ashbee

were killed. One of them however survived that war, and when he started excavating on his own in 1919, he deliberately turned to Pitt-Rivers as his mentor. This young man is the man now full of years and distinction whom we know as Sir Mortimer Wheeler. He and others deliberately turned to Pitt-Rivers and modelled their new techniques on his work and methods. It is not surprising therefore that modern archaeological excavational techniques have a feeling of military and mathematical precision as can be seen looking at Wheeler's own excavations at Stanwick, or at Mr Paul Ashbee's excavations of a round barrow on Salisbury Plain. The cutting of careful sections is one of the key activities of archaeological excavation, which is the surgery of the landscape, the cultural landscape—the section keeps for us the detail of what was cut [51].

Science has not only helped man in the discovery of his past in the present century by providing ways of scientific excavation, but it has also produced all kinds of new techniques—techniques of discovery, techniques of interpretation, and these have added enormously to the way of discovering the past in the last fifty years. I can here only mention a few of these. The first is one that I described earlier—the technique of Carbon 14 dating discovered and developed by Professor Libby in 1945. We now have three Carbon 14 laboratories in England, one in the British Museum, one at the National Physical Laboratory in Teddington and one in the University of Cambridge. There are now no less than 75 of these laboratories scattered all over the world. Their findings are of the greatest value to archaeology and are published each year in a new journal called *Radiocarbon* produced by the American Journal of Science. This journal consists of up-to-date information from all the laboratories and lists of the dates determined by them; it is no exaggeration to say that without these laboratories and their work archaeology would not have advanced by such leaps and bounds as it has in the last twenty years. As I said before, the problem was to find a way of dating the past that was outside man, and took the dates back before man's own first dates of 5000 years

ago. Dendrochronology was some help, and clay varves and pollen analysis even more help; but with radiocarbon dating came a complete break—at last a key to the dating of man's past. C14 dating has been going for only twenty years so far: we can only guess at the answers we shall know in the next twenty years and more. What we shall have is a complete chronological chart of man's past; the real dated past of man will be discovered and charted.

At the beginning of this century an archaeologist was talking to a young man in the late evening of a summer's day: they were seated on the top of a hill in Dorset and looking down at old fields and farms, now long since deserted, that were showing up clearly in the long shadows of the fading light. The archaeologist was Dr Williams-Freeman and the young man O. G. S. Crawford. Williams-Freeman said to Crawford, "You know, archaeologists ought to become birds." Shortly afterwards, in the 1914–18 war men like Crawford did become birds, flew around the countryside, observing the pattern of the past and photographing it. The air camera was able to record the pattern of the ancient cultural landscape that these bird-men saw. From 1920 onwards air photography became one of the great allies of the archaeologist and one of the great discoverers of the past [52].

It discovered the past in two ways; first of all, it showed objects and places and farms and fields and forts and all the rest of the visible cultural landscape in a new and clear light, and one in which they could be understood more easily. When you look at the great hill-fort of Maiden Castle from the air, in the bird-man view (see figure 45 again) you can see at once the interrelation of banks and ditches and the relation of the monument to the surrounding countryside. It is the sort of view and understanding that cannot be obtained on the ground when one is dwarfed by the great banks towering above one. Tara, in Ireland, a site that goes back to the second millennium B.C. but develops in Christian and post-Christian times into one of the great centres of Ireland, is on the ground a complex of earthworks, very difficult to understand when

56. Woodhenge as the monument now is: small concrete posts mark the original post-holes

earthbound! The air photograph shows up all these earthworks: of course they have to be excavated to be dated, but their inter-relations and their relation to the countryside are clearly seen.

But the second and more important help to the archaeologist which the air camera provides is the discovery and recording of sites not visible to or recognisable by the observer on the ground. The monument now referred to as Woodhenge is a good example of such a discovery. In June 1926 Squadron-Leader Insall photographed what he thought was a barrow with curious black dots in it at a site not far from Stonehenge. Excavation

showed that it was not a barrow but a series of concentric holes for wooden posts, a sort of wooden Stonehenge—hence the name Woodhenge. This is just one example of discovery from the air. There are few more exciting moments in archaeology than going into a field holding an air photograph which clearly shows by soil and crop marks the destroyed remains of a barrow or ritual circle, and being quite unable to trace these features on the surface. It is no wonder that people talk of the magic of aerial photography [53].

A third aspect of the working together of science and archaeology is in the analysis of materials— the materials used and fashioned by early man for his tools and weapons. By analysis of stone and flint, of copper and tin, the sources of these raw materials can be traced and the routes along which they were traded found; and so historical facts are found by the petrologist's microscope. A good example of this is provided by Stonehenge itself. It was known for a very long time that there were two kinds of stone employed in the construction of that monument—the very big sarsen stones that had come from north Wiltshire, and the "foreign" or "blue" stones—smaller in size. It was obvious to most observers that they had come from outside Wiltshire but it was not until the late Dr H. H. Thomas of the Geological Survey began work on this problem that the answer was known. Thomas showed that most of the blue stones were of a finely grained igneous rock, a dolerite with occlusions of felspar—it is called a spotted dolerite or nowadays *preselite*, and for a very interesting reason. Dr Thomas found that the only place where this spotted dolerite was found in the British Isles was the northern part of the Preseli Mountains in Pembrokeshire. So science, by petrological analysis and geological mapping, was able to produce a historical, or if you like, a prehistorical fact, namely that the stones, or rather some of the stones, used in the construction of Stonehenge had been brought from Pembrokeshire, a distance of 130 miles as the crow flies [54].

Another fascinating help to the archaeologist has been provided by geophysical prospecting; the detection of buried remains by measurement of the electrical resistivity of the soil is now a well-established technique which has been used for twenty years since, in 1946, Professor Atkinson used the method in his excavation of a group of Neolithic henge monuments at Dorchester in Oxfordshire. Magnetic surveying has now been developed as a very sensitive measuring technique of geophysical prospecting. One of the machines developed is the proton magnetometer which was first used only as recently as 1954. As adapted for archaeological uses the proton-magnetometer can detect such buried remains as iron objects, fired structures such as kilns, furnaces and hearths, pits and ditches filled with top-soil and rubbish, and in special circumstances walls, foundations, roads and graves [55].

And now, archaeology has moved under the

57. Inserting periscope camera in an unopened Etruscan tomb

58. Tomb painting revealed by the periscope camera
(*left*)

59. Byzantine wreck at Yassi Ada—Diver drawing labelled amphoras

sea—a most recent and exciting aspect of archaeological prospecting. The name of Cousteau working under the sea at sites like Le Grand Congloué near Marseilles is well known to most of us. Recently George Bass and others working for the University of Pennsylvania Museum have developed an astonishing technique of archaeology under the water. One of their most famous sites where they developed their techniques of underwater excavation and survey was Cape

66

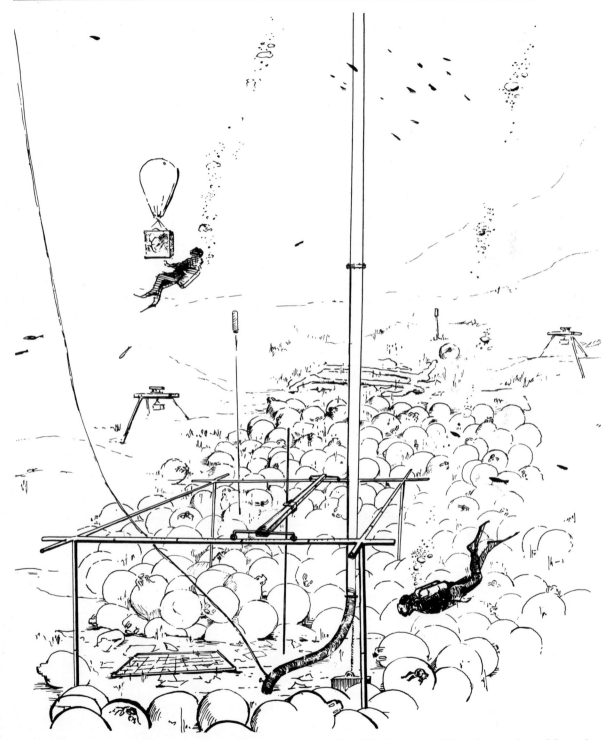

60. Byzantine wreck at Yassi Ada. Plane tables at sides of wreck, with fixed point driven in near bow. Measuring frame and grid placed over tiles of cabin area. Suction pipe is for removing sand, and balloon for lifting objects

part of the world. Archaeology is now a world-wide discipline: it never had any frontiers, now its parish is the world. Archaeology in America has advanced quickly and surely; in no single area has archaeology shown recently such important results as in America, where there have been three big problems, the origin of man in America, the origin of the first peasant village communities in America and the origins of the American civilisations. Now, largely due to C14 research, we know that the first people to enter America came via the Bering Straits somewhere between 30,000 and 20,000 B.C. They were in a state of economy in which they were hunters and fishers, like the people of the Upper Palaeolithic who painted the pictures at Lascaux and Altamira; but the first Americans had no cave art. They spread down from the north of America to the extreme South, and all apparently in a relatively short time.

61. Copán: Mayan monument

Gelidonya off the south coast of Turkey. One of their methods was to place a grid over the wrecked ship they were studying and in the illustration (59) you can see a diver with an aqualung on his back carefully noting, measuring and surveying what he sees on the sea-bottom. At the side there are great piles of amphorae from the wrecked ship. Here is an entirely new and scientific technique, but the University of Pennsylvania did not stop here: they decided to construct an archaeological submarine to assist their reconaissance, survey and excavation under the water, and this they have done. It began to operate in 1964.

Certainly inconceivable in the nineteenth century, and in a kind of way unthought of up to the last quarter century, is the way in which archaeology has extended from the classical areas of study where it developed—Europe and the Middle East and Egypt—to encompass every

62. Copán—Acropolis sculpture of a torch-bearer

63. Ancient Mayan Stele from the ruins at Copán, re-erected in a park in the capital city of Tegucigalpa

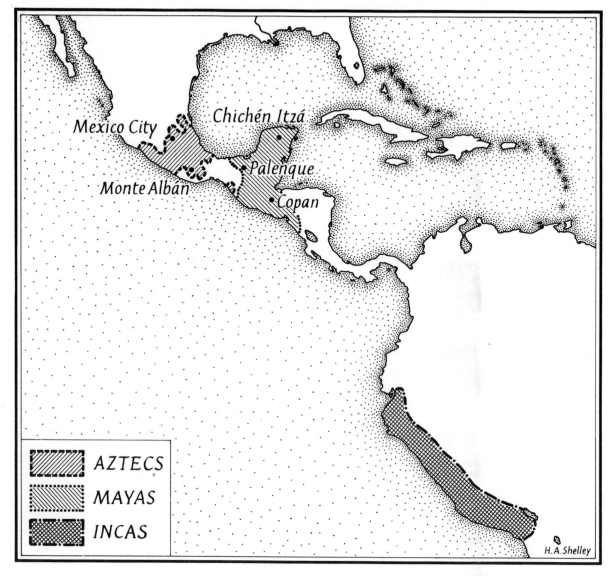

Map 7. Map shewing the distribution of the Aztec, Maya and Inca civilisations

These first Americans remained in a hunting-fishing-foodgathering economy until about 5000 B.C. Then some of them discovered the cultivation of crops: agriculture apparently began in four separate areas of Middle America. Some of the most important researches done on this problem of agricultural origins was done by Professor MacNeish, now of Alberta University, working in Mexico. One of the problems he faced was that although the early central American civilisations were based on maize, no wild maize existed in the world, and yet it was obvious that there had to be wild maize otherwise it could never have been domesticated. By the careful selection of sites—the whole story is one of the most exciting in recent archaeology—MacNeish and others were able to excavate and find what they had been hoping for—to locate wild maize as a fossil plant, and trace its development into a cultivated plant. From this it has been possible to study the growth of proper villages from the earlier incipient agriculture, and the growth of these villages into civilisation itself [57].

This is only one of the many things that has been going on in recent American archaeology. The civilisations that the *conquistadores* found have been studied again: sites like Monte Albán and Mexico City itself and the Mayan sites in Yucatan like Chichen Itza, Palenque and Copán which had been visited a hundred and twenty years ago by Stephens and Catherwood.

The problem brought out into the open by the discovery of four separate centres of agricultural origins in the New World and the apparent development of civilisations in America without notable or perhaps any influence from the old world is an intriguing one, and makes archaeologists and historians think hard about the general problem of cultural origins and the diffusion of culture. This is a fascinating new aspect of man's past that archaeology is forcing us to think about at this moment [58].

Not only in America, but in South-East Asia, Australia, New Zealand, the Pacific and Africa archaeology is giving a new and precise dimension to man's past. One example from South Africa must suffice. We have always known about the mysterious ruins at Zimbabwe in Rhodesia, with a fortress and a ceremonial central area with a curious conical tower. The mystery was, what

64. Zimbabwe—view near the conical towers looking towards the Acropolis—the fortified area on a 200–300 ft. hill rising above the valley

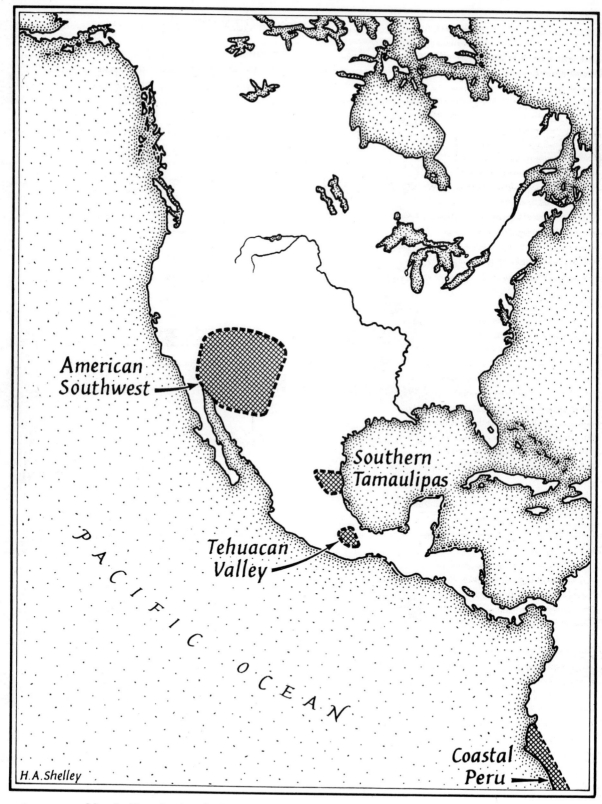

American
Southwest

Southern
Tamaulipas

Tehuacan
Valley

P A C I F I C   O C E A N

Coastal
Peru

H.A.Shelley

Map 8. Map shewing the localities where agriculture was first practised in America

72

relation did these remains have to other ruins of other civilisations? Had the builders of Zimbabwe come from Egypt or Sumeria and when? Was it all B.C. or A.D.? Was Zimbabwe the result of contact with Arabs or was it itself some mysterious ancient civilisation that no-one knew of before? A series of excavations and Carbon 14 dating has resolved this problem and it now looks as though the site itself was occupied as early as the beginning of the Christian era, that it grew and developed at various times certainly under Arab and other outside contacts, but that the conical tower is a construction no earlier than the seventeenth or eighteenth century A.D. [59].

So this is what is happening to us: mystery after mystery is disappearing and we are beginning to build up the true and dated facts about man's early past. Let us in conclusion think back to the story as we have been outlining it in these five short talks. We began with the Assyrian princess doing a little digging, and went on to the mediaeval antiquaries who invented the past, and then the sixteenth and seventeenth century scholars who turned to their written sources, constantly talking about the Druids because this was really all they had at their disposal, and making the Druids the architects of Stonehenge, Avebury and most other prehistoric monuments. Then those who were trying to find dates, like Archbishop Ussher who produced the date 4004 B.C. which for so long dominated the thoughts of many, and their idea of the past of man and the world. Then the great change when scholars began to excavate and find objects and to appreciate that the way to study the past of man was to study his rough stone implements, his polished stone implements, and his artifacts of bronze and iron. In this way a system of the past based on the objects used by man was built up. But it was a system of the past that could not be accurately dated, and for a long while it was a system that was based on excavation that was not scientific and methodical. It is really in the present century that the nineteenth-century system of technological stages which had replaced the guesses of the earlier antiquaries was being replaced by a new system founded on scientific archaeology.

Every generation says it is scientific and that every previous generation was pre-scientific; but I think we can claim honestly and without chance of denial that at present archaeologists are working hard and accurately with a keen sense of purpose, the purpose of recovering the past. By now there is also great achievement: we have by now recovered a great deal of man's early past. When he wrote his book *Primitive Culture* in 1871, Professor E. B. Tylor of Oxford said "The history and prehistory of man now take their proper place in the general scheme of knowledge." I think he was talking a hundred years too soon, and that it is only now that they are beginning to take their proper places in the general scheme of knowledge.

There is still a great deal to do. We have been talking about the discovery of man's past over the last three hundred years. Do not let us suppose that there is not still a great deal to discover. One thing I am sure about: man's past has still a great future.

Notes

[1] For a history of writing see David Diringer, *Writing* (1962), and Maurice Pope, "The Origins of Near Eastern Writing", *Antiquity*, 1966, 17.

[2] On the general history of archaeology see G. E. Daniel, *A Hundred Years of Archaeology* (Third Edition, 1967) and *The Idea of Prehistory* (1962); Stanley Casson, *The Discovery of Man* (1939); Jacquetta Hawkes's Introduction (pp. 3–104) to her large anthology, *The World of the Past* (1963), and Robert F. Heizer's *Man's Discovery of his Past; Literary Landmarks in Archaeology* (Englewood Cliffs, 1962).

[3] On the Greeks and Archaeology see E. D. Phillips, "The Greek Vision of Prehistory", *Antiquity*, 1964, 171.

[4] For an excellent study of mediaeval antiquarianism and the invented past see T. D. Kendrick, *British Antiquity* (1950).

[5] For the legendary history of Oxford and Cambridge see James Parker, *Early History of Oxford* (1885) and Kendrick, op. cit., 25–6.

[6] In his essay on Aubrey in his *Portraits in Miniature* (1931). On Aubrey see J. Collier, *The Scandal and Credulities of John Aubrey* (1931), and A. Powell, *John Aubrey and his Friends* (1948).

[7] For Edward Lhwyd see R. T. Gunther, *Life and Letters of Edward Lhwyd* (1945), which is volume XIV of the series *Early Science in Oxford*.

[8] The standard work on Stukeley is S. Piggott, *William Stukeley* (1950). See also T. D. Kendrick, *The Druids* (1928) and A. L. Owen, *The Famous Druids* (1962).

[9] J. J. A. Worsaae's *Danmarks oldtid oplyst ved Oldsager og Gravhöie* (1942) was translated into English by W. J. Thoms under the title of *The Primeval Antiquities of Denmark* (1849).

[10] On this see G. E. Daniel, *The Three Ages*, (1943), and G. Bibby, *The Testimony of the Spade*, (1957).

[11] The guide was called *Ledetraad til Nordisk Oldkyndighed* and was published in Copenhagen in 1836. The English translation, *A Guide to Northern Antiquities*, translated by Lord Ellesmere, appeared in 1848.

[12] A seventh edition of Lubbock's *Prehistoric Times* (1913) was for sale as a new book in the Cambridge bookshops when I came up as an undergraduate in 1932.

[13] Joseph Déchelette, *Manuel d'archéologie préhistorique* (Paris, 1908), I, 11, and R. A. S. Macalister, *Textbook of European Archaeology* (1921), I, 11.

[14] On the development of classification in the British Museum see T. D. Kendrick, "The British Museum and British Antiquities", *Antiquity*, 1954, 132.

[15] I quote from p. 16 of the Cambridge 1955 edition of the *Religio Medici* by Jean-Jacques Denonain.

[16] J. W. Burgon's dates were 1813–1888. His poem *Petra*, has this couplet:

Match me such marvel save in Eastern clime!
A rose red city 'half as old as time'.

[17] Esper published his finds in 1774 in his *Detailed Report on Recently Discovered Zooliths of Unknown Quadrupeds and the Caves Containing them in the the Upper mountainous countries of the Margravate of Bayreuth*.

[18] For accounts of Buckland and his son Frank see Mrs Godwin's *Life and Correspondence of William Buckland* (1894), George C. Bompas's *Life of Frank Buckland* (1885), and W. Tuckwell *Reminiscences of Oxford* (1907).

[19] A full account of the life and work of John Evans and Arthur Evans will be found in Joan Evans, *Time and Chance* (1943).

[20] A useful guide to these matters of geochronology will be found in F. E. Zeuner's *Dating the Past* (1946).

[21] On the development, uses and problems of C14 dating see Willard F. Libby, *Radiocarbon Dating* (1965—second edition with addenda).

[22] On Napoleon's campaign in Egypt see J. Christopher Herold's *Bonaparte in Egypt* (1963).

[23] For an account of the finding and deciphering of the Rosetta Stone see E. A. Wallis Budge, *The Rosetta Stone* (Revised edition 1950).

[24] Thomas Young's results were published in the 1818 edition of the *Encyclopedia Britannica*. Champollion's decipherment was announced in his famous *Lettre à M. Dacier Relative à l'alphabet des Hiéroglyphes Phonétiques* dated Paris, 22 September, 1822, which is available in translation in C. W. Ceram, *The World of Archaeology* (1966), 162–70.

[25] For the history of archaeological excavation and reconnaissance in Mesopotamia see Seton Lloyd, *Foundations in the Dust* (1947).

[26] Schliemann is best seen through his own books namely *Troy and its Remains* (1875), *Ilios* (1880) *Tiryns* (1880), and *Mycenae* (1878); but see also C. Schuchhardt, *C. Schliemann's Excavations* (1891), Emil Ludwig, *Schliemann: the Story of a Gold-Seeker* (1931), M. Braymer, *The Walls of Windy Troy* (1962) and Lynn and Gray Brooke, *One Passion, Two Loves* (New York, 1966).

[27] Joan Evans's *Time and Chance*, already mentioned, has a good account of her half-brother's excavations in Crete. See also Roland M. Burrows, *The Discoveries in Crete* (1907); J. D. S. Pendlebury, *The Archaeology of Crete* (1939), and R. W. Hutchinson, *Prehistoric Crete* (1962).

[28] Michael Ventris's talk was printed in *The Listener* for July 10, 1952 and is reprinted in Leo Duel's *The Treasures of Time* (1962), 301. See in this connexion John Chadwick's *The Decipherment of Linear B* (1958).

[29] On the discovery of the Hittites see W. Wright, *The Empire of the Hittites* (1884) and A. H. Sayce, *The Hittites: the Story of a Forgotten Empire* (1888). Also see O. R. Gurney, *The Hittites* (1952).

[30] On the Indus Civilisation see S. Piggott, *Prehistoric India* (1950), and R. E. M. Wheeler, *Early India and Pakistan* (1959); *The Indus Civilisation* (1960, 2nd ed.); *Civilizations of the Indus Valley and Beyond* (1966).

[31] For early China see W. Watson, *China before the Han Dynasty* (1961), Chêng Tê-k'un, *Shang China* (1960), and Li Chi, *The Beginnings of Chinese Civilisation* (Seattle, 1957).

[32] For a general account of these problems see Rushton Coulborn, *The Origin of Civilised Societies* (Princeton, 1959), and G. E. Daniel, *Archaeology and the Origins of Civilisation* (1967).

[33] The story of the discovery of Upper Palaeolithic art is well told in Colin-Simard, *Découverte archéologique de la France* (Paris, 1955), H. Breuil, *Four Hundred Centuries of Cave-Art*, (Montignac, 1952) and M. C. Burkitt, *Prehistory* (1925).

[34] For an account of the restoration work at Lascaux see *Paris Match* for January 2, 1965 and *Antiquity*, 1965, 82.

[35] Gordon Childe's views were first clearly set out in his *Man Makes Himself* (1936) and developed in *What Happened in History* (1954, revised edition).

[36] Breasted developed the idea of "the Fertile Crescent" in J. H. Breasted, *Ancient Times: A History of the Early World* (Boston, 1916). See particularly Chapter IV and the map between pages 102 and 103.

[37] On these matters see (ed.) R. J. Braidwood and G. R. Willey *Courses Toward Urban Life* (Chicago, 1962), H. Frankfort, *The Birth of Civilisation in the Near East* (New York, 1956) and J. Mellaart, *The Earliest Civilisations of the Near East* (1965).

[38] On Jericho see M. Wheeler, *The Walls of Jericho* (1956) K. Kenyon, *Digging up Jericho* (1957) and *Archaeology in the Holy Land* (1960); E. Anati, *Palestine Before the Hebrews* (London, 1963); G. Ernest Wright, *Biblical Archaeology* (Revised edition, 1962).

[39] For a general account of megalithic monuments see G. E. Daniel, *The Megalith-Builders of Western Europe* (1958) and S. P. ORíordáin and Glyn Daniel, *New Grange and the Bend of the Boyne* (1964).

[40] On West Kennet itself S. Piggott, *The West Kennet Long Barrow Excavations 1955–6* (1962) and *The Neolithic Cultures of the British Isles* (1954); G. E. Daniel, *The Prehistoric Chamber Tombs of England and Wales* (1950).

[41] The best and only up-to-date account of this great stone circle is R. J. C. Atkinson, *Stonehenge* (1956).

[42] For an up-to-date account of prehistoric Europe see S. Piggott, *Ancient Europe from the beginnings of Agriculture to Classical Antiquity* (1965).

[43] R. E. M. Wheeler, *Maiden Castle, Dorset* (1943).

[44] A good general account of the Vix find is in R. Joffroy, *Le trésor de Vix* (Paris, 1962).

[45] R. Martin, "Wooden Figures from the Source of the Seine", *Antiquity*, 1965, 247.

[46] For a good general account of the finding of the Viking Ships see Geoffrey Bibby, *The Testimony of the Spade* (New York, 1956), chapter 24. The whole of the March, 1940 issue of *Antiquity* was devoted to the Sutton Hoo find.

[47] This is quoted from Bishop Otter's *Life of E. D. Clarke*, 505.

[48] The full title of Belzoni's book was *A Narrative of the Operations and Recent Discoveries within the Pyramids, Temples, Tombs and Excavations in Egypt and Nubia; and of a Journey to the Coast of the Red Sea in search of the Ancient Berenice; and another to the Oasis of Jupiter Ammon* and it was published in 1821. For a good account of Belzoni's life and work see M. Willson Disher, *Pharaoh's Fool* (1957).

[49] Sir Flinders Petrie's autobiography, *Seventy Years in Archaeology* was published in 1931.

[50] No life of General Pitt-Rivers has yet been written, but there is an interesting memoir of him by H. St George Gray in Volume V of the *Excavations in Cranborne Chase*. The first four volumes in this series were written by the General; the fifth published posthumously in 1905.

[51] On excavation in general see R. E. M. Wheeler, *Archaeology from the Earth* (1954) and R. J. C. Atkinson, *Field Archaeology* (1946).

[52] There are various versions of this story. See O. G. S. Crawford's autobiography, *Said and Done* (1955).

[53] The Woodhenge photographs were discussed and published by Mrs M. E. Cunnington, in her article "Prehistoric Timber Circles", *Antiquity*, 1927, 92.

[54] For this and other aspects of research on Stonehenge see R. J. C. Atkinson, *Stonehenge* (1956).

[55] For an account of this and other geophysical techniques used by archaeologists see M. J. Aitken, *Physics and Archaeology* (1961).

[56] George Bass, *Archaeology Under Water* (1966).

[57] On this see R. J. Braidwood, *The Near East and the Foundation for Civilisation* (Eugene, 1952), and J. G. D. Clark and S. Piggott, *Prehistoric Societies* (1966), and J. G. D. Clark, *World Prehistory* (1961).

[58] For a summary of MacNeish's views see R. S. MacNeish "The Origins of American Agriculture", *Antiquity*, 1965, 87. See also for up-to-date accounts of American origins G. H. S. Bushnell, *Peru* (Second edition, 1965) M. Coe, *Mexico* (1962) and *The Mayas* (1967), and Betty J. Meggers, *Ecuador* (1966).

[59] On Zimbabwe see Roger Summers *Zimbabwe, a Rhodesian Mystery* (1963) and G. Caton-Thompson, "Zimbabwe, All Things Considered", *Antiquity*, 1964, 99.

Books for Further Reading

The notes contain detailed references to certain topics including the history of archaeology. To those listed in note 2 may be added T. K. Penniman, *A Hundred Years of Anthropology* (Third, revised edition, 1965), A. Michaelis, *A Century of Archaeological Discovery* (1908), C. W. Ceram, *Gods, Graves and Scholars* (1952) and *A Picture History of Archaeology* (1958) and *Archaeology* (1965).

The following are anthologies of archaeology: Margaret Wheeler, *A Book of Archaeology: Seventeen Stories of Discovery* (1957) and *A Second Book of Archaeology* (1959); Leo Duel, *The Treasures of Time* (1961); R. F. Heizer, *The Archaeologist at Work* (1959) and *Man's Discovery of his Past: Literary Landmarks in Archaeology;* R. F. Jessup, *Curiosities of British Archaeology;* Jacquetta Hawkes, *The World of the Past* (1963) and C. W. Ceram, *The World of Archaeology* (1966). A good anthology dealing only with American archaeology is Robert Wauchope, *They Found the Buried Cities* (1965).

Books providing an introduction to archaeology include Grahame Clark, *Archaeology and Society* (1957); S. Piggott, *Aspects of Archaeology* (1959); Mortimer Wheeler, *Archaeology from the Earth* (1954); S. De Laet, *Archaeology and its Problems* (1957); Kathleen Kenyon, *Beginning in Archaeology* (new edition, 1964); and F. Hole and R. F. Heizer, *An Introduction to Prehistoric Archaeology* (1965). Among the few books that give a general synthesis of prehistory we may mention, Grahame Clark, *World Prehistory* (1961); G. Clark and S. Piggott, *Prehistoric Societies* (1965); (ed.) S. Piggott, *The Dawn of Civilisation* (1961); and V. Gordon Childe, *What Happened in History* (1960) and *Man Makes Himself* (1936).

Books on how to get to archaeological sites include Jacquetta Hawkes, *Guide to the Prehistoric and Roman Monuments in England and Wales* (1951); Nicholas Thomas, *A Guide to Prehistoric England* (1960); Richard Feachem, *Prehistoric Scotland* (1963); S. P. ORíordáin, *The Antiquities of the Irish Countryside* (1953); G. E. Daniel, *The Hungry Archaeologist in France* (1964); the series of Regional Guides produced by Cory, Adams and Mackay (e.g. Houlder and Manning, *South Wales*, 1966); and the Faber series of Archaeological Guides of which the first, *Sicily*, by Margaret Guido will appear in 1967.

The autobiographies of archaeologists make good reading: here are some—Leonard Woolley, *Spadework* (1953); Mortimer Wheeler, *Still Digging* (1955); Margaret Murray, *My First Hundred Years* (1964); Flinders Petrie, *Seventy Years in Archaeology* (1931); E. A. Wallis Budge, *By Nile and Tigris* (1920); O. G. S. Crawford, *Said and Done* (1955); J. Beddoe, *Memories of Eighty Years* (1910).

For a good treatment of some of the scientific aspects of archaeology mentioned in the fifth lecture see (eds.) D. Brothwell and E. Higgs, *Science in Archaeology* (1963); and (ed.) E. Pyddoke, *The Scientist and Archaeology* (1963).

Important Dates

1650 Sir William Dugdale's *History of Warwickshire*
Ussher's *Annals of the Ancient and New Testaments*

1795 Finding of the Rosetta Stone

1797 John Frere's letter to the Society of Antiquaries of London

1809–13 *Description de l'Egypte*

1819 Danish National Museum opened, organised on the three age system by C. J. Thomsen

1820 Belzoni's *Narrative of the Operations and Recent Discoveries within the Pyramids, Temples, Tombs, and Excavations in Egypt and Nubia*

1830–33 Sir Charles Lyell, *Principles of Geology*

1836 *Ledetraad til Nordisk Oldkyndighed* (English translation in 1848 entitled *Guide to Northern Antiquities*)

1842 Stephens and Catherwood describe the Maya remains

1847 Rawlinson records the Behistun inscription

1853 Swiss Lake dwellings discovered at Obermeilen

1859 Authenticity of man's antiquity affirmed in London and Aberdeen. Publication of Charles Darwin's *Origin of Species*

1860 Lartet at Massat

1865 Lubbock's *Prehistoric Times*

1871 Schliemann begins excavations at Troy

1875 Lartet and Christy *Reliquiae Aquitanicae*
De Sautuola begins work at Altamira

1877 De Sarzec at Telloh

1880 Pitt-Rivers begins work on Cranborne Chase

1896 Rivière at La Mouthe

1901 Discovery of Font-de-Gaume and Les Combarelles

1902 A.F.A.S. meeting at Montauban and afterwards at La Mouthe. Cartailhac's *Mea culpa d'un sceptique*

1906 Niaux discovered

1924 Mohenjo-daro and Harappa revealed as prehistoric cities

1926 Excavation of Tutankhamen's tomb and the Royal Graves at Ur

1928 Excavations begin at Anyang
Crawford and Keiller, *Wessex from the Air*

1940 Discovery of Lascaux

1946 Professor Willard Libby announces the C14 method

1950 Piggott-Atkinson excavations begin at Stonehenge

1953 Vix burial found

1963 Professor Martin finds wooden figures at the source of the Seine

Index